The Rise of
NEW KIDS ON THE BLOCK...
and
A GUY NAMED MAURICE STARR
Before the Legend - The Early Years

(An Unauthorized Biography)

What the Media Had To Say…

They may no longer be new. They may no longer be kids. But NKOTB just might be out to prove they still have the right stuff.… New Kids on the Block, the prototypical boy band of the 1980s and early '90s that preceded the Backstreet Boys and 'N Sync on the pop charts and in the pages of Tiger Beat, are reportedly on track to reunite.
—**E! Online**

The boy band New Kids on the Block, which sold 70 million albums in the 1980s and early '90s, has reunited and plans to release a new album and go on tour. The reunion comes 20 years after the release of the group's multiplatinum album, "Hanging Tough."
—**ASSOCIATED PRESS**

Yes, much has changed since 1993, the last time the NKOTB performed together, and until recently few would have taken the bet that we would have ever seen the quintet at it again.
—**MTV.COM**

The New Kids on the Block took Westwood, a small Boston suburb, by storm. It helped that they were hometown boys. Bad-boy Donnie Wahlberg and jockish Danny Wood grew up in the grizzled Boston neighborhood of Dorchester. Front-man Jordan Knight and his brother Jonathan were born in Worcester. The baby, Joey (who is now 36!), grew up in Jamaica Plain. To the kids of Westwood, these guys were bigger than Aerosmith, bigger than Bobby Brown—even bigger than the Red Sox!
—**TODAY SHOW.COM**

(May 2008) the New Kids on the Block caused fan mayhem when they resurfaced on the Today show on a windy and rainy New York morning, and similarly dreary conditions awaited the estimated 4,000 who crowded into the show's plaza early today for the five singers' first performance together in 15 years.
—**ROLLING STONE**

The Commonwealth of Massachusetts

The House of Representatives

Citation

Be it hereby known to all that:
The Massachusetts House of Representatives
hereby offers its sincerest congratulations to:

TONY ROSE
Hit City Recording Studio

in recognition of

**His Outstanding Commitment to
Neighborhood and Community Leadership**

The entire membership extends its very best wishes
and expresses the hope for future good fortune
and continued success in all endeavors.

Given this 15th day of OCTOBER 1988
at the State House, Boston, Massachusetts

by: _____

George Keverian
Speaker of The House

Offered by: _____
SHIRLEY OWENS-HICKS
State Representative

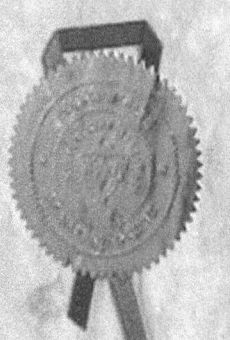

The Rise of
NEW KIDS ON THE BLOCK...
and
A GUY NAMED MAURICE STARR
Before the Legend - The Early Years

(An Unauthorized Biography)

By: Tony Rose

Colossus Books
Phoenix   New York
Los Angeles

The Rise of
NEW KIDS ON THE BLOCK...
and
A GUY NAMED MAURICE STARR
Before the Legend - The Early Years

(An Unauthorized Biography)

BY: TONY ROSE

Published by:
Colossus Books
A Division of Amber Communications Group, Inc.
1334 East Chandler Boulevard, Suite 5-D67
Phoenix, AZ 85048
Amberbk@amberbooks.com
WWW.AMBERBOOKS.COM

ALL RIGHTS RESERVED

No part of this book may be used, reproduced or transmitted in any form or by any means—electronic or mechanical, including photocopying, recording or by any information storage and retrieved system without written permission from the author, except for the inclusion of brief quotations in a review or critical article.

COLOSSUS BOOKS are available at special discounts for bulk purchases, sales promotions, fund raising or educational purposes.

The Rise of New Kids On the Block...and a Guy Named Maurice Starr : The Early Years Before the Legend - The Early Years (An Unauthorized Biography)

Copy right © 1995, 2008 by Conant Rose

Writers Guild of America Registration: 1995, 2008

Paperback ISBN: 979-8-8690-8630-3

Hardcover ISBN: 979-8-8691-0002-3

Library of Congress Control Number: 2024900696

Dedication

To the Boston/Roxbury Music Scene: All the Musicians, Players, Groups, Bands, Friends, Girls I knew 'back in the day', Maurice Starr, Prince Charles and the City Beat Band, Larry "Woo" Wedgeworth, Slyck, The Jonzun Crew, New Edition, New Kids On The Block, and my main man EDMON...IT WAS THE REEL THANG.

—LOVE YOU ALL. FOREVER, TONY

The Rise of New Kids on the Block...

Acknowledgments

To Maurice Starr, Charles Alexander, Michael Johnson and Yvonne Rose…all who I met in Roxbury, Mass., 1979. You changed my life forever; I hope I did the same for you.

To Kay Bourne and Melvin B. Miller, who wrote about us, gave us space, and our careers in the "Bay State Banner".

To Kendall A. Minter, Esq. (Minter & Associates), "my brother", my friend.

To Eleanor Blockington…thank you.

To Elvin, Donnie and Calvin…I'll never forget you guys.

To the parents of New Kids on the Block…for believing in Maurice Starr and Roxbury.

And to Ray Johnson, Sr. and Willie Mae Johnson who began it all.

God bless all of you…

Tony Rose
Phoenix, AZ
2008

The Rise of New Kids on the Block...

Contents

Foreword xiii

Preface xvii

The Beginning. xxi

America Is Still the Land of Great Opportunity. xxiii

Introduction 1

Part One. The Roots of a Legend 3
   Chapter One. Donnie 5
   Chapter Two. Jordan 11
   Chapter Three. Jonathan 19
   Chapter Four. Danny. 23
   Chapter Five. Joey 27

Part Two. Maurice Starr 35
   Chapter Six. The Johnson Family Foundation 37
   Chapter Seven. The Genius Emerges 45
   Chapter Eight. The Road To Riches 49
   Chapter Nine. Paying Dues. 55

Part Three. The Boston Music Scene 61
   Chapter Ten. A New Base Is Built In Boston 63
   Chapter Eleven. Maurice Starr Emerges to the Forefront . . . 69
   Chapter Twelve. The Legend Begins—
      The Birth of Boston International Records 71
   Chapter Thirteen. Breaking Into The Big Time. 73
   Chapter Fourteen. The Story Unfolds 85
   Chapter Fifteen. Fall From Grace. 95

Part Four. The Building of an Empire 99
    Chapter Sixteen. The Evolution Begins 101
    Chapter Seventeen. The Search Is On 105
    Chapter Eighteen. Hard Work Prevails 111
    Chapter Nineteen. Getting In The Door 115
    Chapter Twenty. Fate Takes An Upper Hand 121
    Chapter Twenty-One. The Struggle Continues 123
    Chapter Twenty-Two. Taking A Stand. 127
    Chapter Twenty-Three. A Step Closer 133

Conclusion 139

New Kids On the Block Albums & Singles 141

Let The Touring Begin: 147

Index 149

About the Author 159

Foreword

In 1953 many legends were born, but only one musical genius would create an international frenzy with a group of boys from North Dorchester and Jamaica Plain in Boston. Larry Johnson would become Maurice Starr, sur rounded by love and music from day one, and des tined to become a hit-making song writer and producer responsible for culminating 70 million record sales world wide.

The Rise of New Kids on the Block…and a Guy Named Maurice Starr: Before the Legend - The Early Years is a remarkable true story as told by author Tony Rose, the primary architect along with Maurice Starr of the Boston/Roxbury Music Scene. When the fairy tale began, like a cosmic force, the entities were des tined by fate to be in place where the dream would unfold.

There had been a seed planted within the heart of the six foot three African American musician and a mission instilled in him to journey north from Deland, Florida. The journey was full of ups and downs, laughter and tears, hand shakes and controversy… never the less, it ended up in a place called Roxbury…the place where Tony was born and returned to…the place that Maurice settled in…. the place where Donnie, Jordan, Jon a than, and Danny would go to school…the place that would become the birthplace of the New Kids on the Block.

Meeting Tony Rose was like entering a new world of fireworks, fast cars, and passionate music beats…I was in fashion and had not witnessed the music scene firsthand… until that day. I had no idea where this would all lead to, or that December 27, 1979, would be recorded in the Bay State Banner by "The Scoop" as a part of Boston's music history.

In 1980, Tony Rose and Yvonne (Willis) Rose became known as the "Terrible 2."

We were at the height of the party when the six-foot-four warrior dressed in a full-length fox fur coat, topped by a felt fedora filled the frame of the doorway at Club 51. Tony Rose was followed by his entourage, Prince Charles and the City Beat Band, Maurice Starr, Prince Charles Alexander, Dr. Funkenchain, and Sargent Funk. Record Producers, Tony Rose, Maurice Starr, and Producer/Artist Prince Charles Alexander had just completed "IN THE STREETS", which was number one on full rotation at WILD, Roxbury (Boston's) #1 Black Radio Station and they were hooking up at Club 51 to party and celebrate after Maurice finished his gig at Doc's. Tony and I, Yvonne (Willis) Rose, would soon become known as the "TERRIBLE 2".

Foreword

Tony and Maurice were best friends…they met in 1979…they became tight…like brothers. Maurice shared his adventures and musical techniques with Tony. Tony shared his adventures, marketing and promotional techniques with Maurice. But fate would eventually set them on separate paths—Tony who was into the funk and rap would set up an international recording and production company and move to New York and London—Maurice would be into R & B and rap and build up an international recording and production company in Roxbury. When Tony returned to Roxbury and built a recording studio in 1988, he and Maurice would begin working together again.

Maurice was on a mission to impact the music world with a boy group and did just that with the New Edition until the unspeakable happened…. and they were gone. They say when something bad hap pens it just opens the door for some thing bigger and better.

Tony Rose was right on the scene when Maurice Starr began to move and maneuver toward his des tiny… the des tiny that would ultimately create the international phenom e non…New Kids on the Block. Tony tells the story brilliantly, from the beginning to the end, starting with each Kid's family history and street credibility, and including Maurice's musical roots and upbringing that would ultimately enable him to have the knowledge and discipline to undertake and complete their journey. The book is like the fairy tale that it is, encompassing all the great ness that Maurice Starr instilled in the historical boy group movement and the intense determination spirited by the New Kids on the Block's desire to succeed.

But, unlike Menudo, the New Kids were keepers…they would maintain their places in the group until they dis banded…and realizing that age is nothing but a number…they're back!

Tony Rose has left no stone unturned…it's all here…I know…I was a witness.

—Yvonne Rose

The Rise of New Kids on the Block...

Preface

It was early 1975, I had been working in the A & R department at RCA Records, Los Angeles and had signed an act (Robbie Hill and the Family Affair) to my management company Nova Productions. RCA's number one R&B singing group, the Main Ingredient whose lead singer was Cuba Gooding (you know his son, the actor Cuba Gooding, Jr.) came out to Los Angeles to set up, record and tour. I went to Don Berkheimer, head of A&R at RCA Records and inquired about signing my group to RCA to do a couple of singles and he said "Yes, but why don't you sign them through Cuba Gooding and Luther Simmons." RCA had just given the Main Ingredient (Cuba and Luther) their own production deal through Super Group Productions, which would be distributed by RCA Records. So, I went to Cuba and he said, "Sure, let's hear them."

In the meantime, the Main Ingredient needed a band to accompany them on tour, so Robbie Hill and the Family Affair became the Main Ingredient's band for their tour and I went on to become their tour manager. Eventually I went on to sign the group with Super Group Productions to be distributed by RCA Records. I had been living out in Los Angeles for a few years and had worked at The Burbank Studios (Warner Brothers and Columbia Pictures) Warner/Electra/Atlanta Records, Warren Lanier Public Relations and RCA Records and knew most of the people at RCA Records, East and West coast, and most of the major record labels in Los Angeles and New York.

The Rise of New Kids on the Block...

In 1977, during one of my trips back to Boston, I saw a group called the Energetics, and shortly after, met with their manager Roscoe Gorham. I told Roscoe that if he had any tapes I would take them back to Los Angeles with me and would shop them around to see if there were any buyers/deals I could get for the group. So, I took the tapes back to Los Angeles and got the Energetics a distribution deal with a small label. They paid $8000 for the tapes, and Roscoe paid me 10% of it.

While making the deal, across the hall working in a small studio was the legendary Motown producer/songwriter Brian Holland, so I went over to say "Hi". He asked me what I was doing there. I told him I was closing a deal for some tapes that I had from a group in Boston called the Energetics. So, he said he knew the group and had been interested in them. I told him I would let the group's manager Roscoe Gorham know. So I did, and Roscoe and Brian got together; and Brian signed the group to an album deal with Atlantic Records, which came out in 1979.

In 1979, I was back in Boston, and during a blizzard I was listening to the radio and heard a song called "Bout Time I Funk You." The announcer came on and said that the guy who was just on was Maurice Starr and that he would be appearing at a club called Corteez on Washington Street in Dorchester. At the time, I was living in Dorchester right up the street from Corteez on Talbot Avenue....so I went to check him out.

When I met Maurice Starr that February night we formed an instant bond. We were both on the verge of finding something...doing something big...and we felt it. Together we had a special energy...his to me, mine to him. He also knew that I had done that deal for the Energetics and that was giving me big credibility. He introduced me to his set in Roxbury/Dorchester, at all the clubs, we hung out, came over to my place and we talked.

We were giving each other that energy we needed to move to the next level. Soon we started going out, doing television shows, radio interviews, promoting the record. Maurice had originally put his record out ('Bout Time I Funk You') on his own Boston International Records label. I did a lot of work to help him, including talking to the people in A&R at RCA Records like Jerome Gasper, Wendell Bates, Ron Mosley, and eventually the record and Maurice did get signed to RCA Records and we went on tour.

I became like his road manager and worked with him touring in Buffalo, NY, Cleveland, places like that. In his band was a young guy named Charles Alexander. While on tour, Charles mentioned that he had a song sketch called "In the Streets" and asked if I would work with him on it. Michael Jonzun (Maurice's brother) also heard the song and mentioned that it might be something that I might want to get involved with. Maurice laid down some killer bass, guitar lines and production, I did some work on it, Charles laid down his lead vocals, some flute and funky bass lines on this Lyricon he had and Michael laid down the backbeat, did some more work on it, took it in the studio and mixed it down for us.

So, I put out the record "In the Streets" on my Solid Platinum Records and Productions label in October 1979. I distributed it, promoted it, marketed it, publicized it, got it on the radio and sold it all over America and eventually all over the world. With RCA Records pushing "Bout Time I Funk You" nationally all over the United States with Maurice's name as producer and songwriter and with me pushing "In the Streets" by Prince Charles and the City Beat Band on my Solid Platinum Records and Productions with myself, Charles Alexander (who I would manage and co-produce with for ten years), Michael Jonzun and Maurice Starr as producers/songwriters and me also as executive producer, it began and gave us the careers we'd all been looking for. It put us all on a national level. I made "In The Streets" a major record that propelled all of us eventually to international fame, it got our names out there. At that time, I had known Maurice for exactly nine months....we became friends for life.

—Tony Rose

The Rise of New Kids on the Block...

The Beginning......

"Some people think we have no talent and that Maurice is the Crook Svengali Puppeteer, and that's a lot of garbage. Especially with kid acts, people think there's got to be evil stage parents or evil, greedy adults behind you. We're not Menudo. Danny's not going to get replaced if he grows a mustache. We do have the talent to produce, and write, and play, and we will do more of it. We've done some on records already... But right now we're still learning, still growing, we're proud of our past. And we're confident of our future. We know people are going to try and stick drugs in our faces—do something to trip us up. But we're not worried. We know who we are, and we're not puppets. There are no strings".
—Donnie Wahlberg -November 2nd 1989

"These are like my own kids. I practically raised these guys. I couldn't feel closer to my own kids."
—Maurice Starr—1989

"Maurice has been like a father to us. He's been our biggest influence".
—Jonathan Knight—1989

"They needed to learn to dance. The group rehearsed in Dorchester at a place called the Lee School, a community center for black kids. I put the group there to see black talent, to feel the vibe. That's where the kids learned dancing and singing. You can be black and not be convincing; but to be white, you have to be 1000 times more convincing, so it was work. I made sure they made the right moves. I wanted regular guys, so they dressed themselves. But I put them with the right type of people...

The Rise of New Kids on the Block...

black choreographers, for instance. Singing, they had to have a certain tone. When Joe first came in he had an operatic voice. So, I got him a Michael Jackson album and told him to listen to the way he phrases, the way he handles the vibrato, from when to open or close their mouths, when to sing and not to sing vibrato, from A to Z. I went over it all."
—***Maurice Starr—March 11, 1990***

America is Still the Land of Great Opportunity...

On July 20th, 21st, 23rd and 24th at a sold out Giants Stadium, (1990), the New Kids On The Block, with their producer Maurice Starr, made a triumphant entrance into New York City. Their lives had been filled with hard work, determination, dedication, confidence, success and many failures, but they never lost their belief, love, and loyalty for one another. Theirs is a history, filled with respect for people of all backgrounds, cultures and colors, black, white, yellow, red, brown, rappers, soul, funk, blues, rock, dancing, singing, back alleys and the mean streets of Boston.

Five working-class boys living in the "blue collar districts" of Boston, called North Dorchester and Jamaica Plain, and a record producer from Roxbury would go to the dizzying heights of the music world at a speed so phenomenal, that it shattered most existing record sales and concert tour sales.

From the bottom, to the top, this is the true, undoctored, hard-hitting, fact-filled story of Donnie Wahlberg, Jordan Knight, Jonathan Knight, Danny Wood, and Joe McIntyre......New Kids On The Block......and a guy named Maurice Starr.

Come with me and let me tell you the true story, the real story, the only story. I was there....

Tony Rose

The Rise of New Kids on the Block...

Introduction

America was changing. The Vietnam war was at its peak. Jimi Hendrix, The Doors and The Beatles ruled the music world. Man had made "one step forward for humanity" on the moon and Boston's Mayor Kevin White was interested in bringing Boston's racially segregated neighborhoods together.

Growing up in North Dorchester, a town of 70,000 people, would not have been easy; for it was bordered on one side by Roxbury/Dorchester/Mattapan—an all Black section of Boston where welfare, crime, poor housing, bad education and drugs dominated—and on another side by South Boston—an all White section of Boston where welfare, crime, poor housing, bad education, and alcoholism dominated. All of these conditions could, and did, destroy many young minds; and they might have had a very negative effect on the New Kids on The Block, but a number of things were in Donnie's, Danny's, Jordan's, Jonathan's and Joey's favor.

North Dorchester was like a free zone where black families and white Families, black kids and white kids (though not overly friendly towards one another) did have a healthy respect for each other and one another's culture. Though Jeremiah Burke and Dorchester High were predominantly White schools, most families had kids who had gone there with, as they called them in the sixties, "the colored". Because of skin color, religion, and culture, the North Dorchester kids closely resembled those of South Boston; but, they did not experience the intense poverty, segregated education, broken families, or racial hatred suffered by the South Boston people.

Oh, there were fights and bad words were sometimes passed between both races, but the people of North Dorchester, Dorchester, and sometimes Roxbury, did communicate and did learn from one another. And, in that learning, each took some of the more positive and stronger attributes. The whites learned how to dance better, sing better, and later, rap. They would learn meditation, and how to live and relate to people of other cultures. And, the blacks would learn more about how the city's system worked, a lot about the Boston Red Sox, and how to trust people from another culture.

Thus, when the city of Boston was ordered by a federal judge to desegregate all of Boston's public schools by sending white kids to all black schools, and black kids to all white schools, kids from North Dorchester—like Donnie, Danny, Jonathan and Jordan—had no problem, because their parents had no problem. As Donnie says, "We grew up when they were trying to integrate the city through bussing." Some people have even said 'ha, they even went to black schools to train to be black,' as if it was an intricate plan. We learned a lot of very positive things, and got good educations. So much for the racists out there who say black and white kids can't go to school together".

Part One
The Roots of a Legend

The Rise of New Kids on the Block...

Chapter One
Donnie

Donnie E. Wahlberg, a Leo, was born August 17, 1969. His parents Alma and Donald had eight other children: Debbie, Michele, Arthur, Paul, James, Tracey, Robert and the youngest Mark. Donnie was called "Baby Donnie" by his mother. His father's name was Donald, Sr.

Donnie was born with sandy blonde hair and hazel eyes into a large loving family. Donald, Sr., a strong father figure, drove trucks and Alma, a fun-loving pretty blonde woman, worked hard keeping her large brood together. She loved music and always had music playing in the house. Alma performed in a lot of parish church musicals at St. Elizabeth's Church in Dorchester, and was in a mother's dance group. She was a great inspiration to Donnie. Growing as a child, older Donnie became a peacemaker. He didn't like arguments and probably got his strong sense of justice from mediating his brothers' and sisters' fights.

Buying gifts for loved ones was a big deal for Donnie. One time he noticed that his mother liked to watch "60 Minutes", especially, the "Andy Rooney" segment. That Christmas Donnie gave his mother an Andy Rooney book.

As a child Donnie was very energetic—always on the go. But, he always was concerned and caring about his friends and family. Being sensitive, he'd worry if someone was hurt or crying. Donnie always genuinely cared about people, and they would care about him.

Donnie was different from the other kids. He demanded attention when he spoke, and everyone listened. He loved music and was always banging around on things. Yet, Donnie was creative, always drawing, and writing short stories; and he had a great imagination.

When Donnie started school, kids from North Dorchester had to go to school in Roxbury and kids from Roxbury went to schools in South Boston—in other words, the white kids went to all black schools and black kids went to all white schools. At these schools, beginning in kindergarten, Donnie met Danny, Jordan, and Jonathan. They were also being bussed, and their roots and families were based in North Dorchester too. At these schools, they met kids from other backgrounds and learned to respect and enjoy them. Because they started going to school early with black kids, they had no fear of, or prejudice against people from other cultures. As Donnie stated, "Outside of meeting Maurice Starr, going to school with black kids was the best thing to ever happen to us. We learned a lot and got good educations."

This early introduction to black people probably explains why when meeting Maurice Starr, Donnie who was the first one to meet him, was comfortable and Maurice would see right away that he had soul and was funky… and dreams and fate would meet.

Donnie lived a normal life with his family, attending school, playing baseball with his brothers Jimbo, Bobbo and Mark, and competing with them to see who was the better athlete, and later for girls. His mother's heart would burst with pride when young Donnie received his first Holy Communion. Dressed in white, she reflected "Donnie looked like an angel". Donnie grew up loving his large family, especially the way his father cooked, and he never left the house without telling his mother he loved her, and was never ashamed or embarrassed to kiss his brothers and sisters. Donnie is a very open person.

Donnie and his family did know hard times. With nine kids and two adults, there were a lot of people to feed. Donald, Sr. would drive trucks and cook to earn a living. He would then bring food home and cook it with all the family gathered around feeling good. Smelling one of Donald, Sr.'s great sizzling steaks or his out-of-this-world spaghetti sauce, was another reason why Donnie loved his father's cooking. Although the family had hard times, with Donald, Sr.'s and Alma's love you didn't even know it.

"It was great", Alma recalled. "I thought that everyone had nine children and everyone lived the way we did. When I look at them all together, I think, it has all worked out and I'm pretty proud of all of them."

As you can guess, Christmas was the biggest time of the year at all the New Kids houses; and Donnie's was no exception. Christmas Eve, they'd all gather at the top of the stairs and just sit there waiting for Christmas morning, getting excited and hugging each other. Finally, when their parents would get up, they'd go crazy, fly down the stairs, and the nine of them would start ripping open their presents. As they grew older, tons and tons of kids would be flying all over the house; and Donnie, Danny, Jordan, Jonathan and (after they became New Kids) Joey would visit each others houses mixing in with all the other kids making a huge noise every Christmas in North Dorchester.

Donnie loved his childhood—meeting new friends, hanging with his brothers and playing lots of Little League Baseball. He enjoyed playing with his Teddy, his army men, and all the toys little boys have to have, especially the Sesame Street characters Grover and Big Bird. He made comic books, and they would be about outer space characters—all kinds of little characters.

Donnie had a swell and determined nature. If he wanted something he'd go after it—something he got from his father. Donnie's first kiss with a girl came when he was eight. He and the girl were hiding behind a dumpster, and her brother caught them. The girl's brother was a little older than Donnie, and he started telling the whole neighborhood. So "Dennis Cheese" (Donnie), like his favorite cartoon character Dennis the Menace, ran into the house and didn't come back out. Even when the ice cream truck came, Donnie was too embarrassed to come outside. The next day, Donnie and the girl were discovered kissing in the pool. When Donnie came home, his family was in the front room, and all at the same time they chanted "kissing in the pool" and handsome Donnie gave them his "cheese smile".

At thirteen, Donnie got serious and decided he was going to be famous. By this time, he had formed a neighborhood band and he would bang on anything and everything instructing the other kids on what they should be doing. Getting his stance from the black kids at school, Donnie started wearing sunglasses and "hangin' tough".

Rap was just beginning to hit the cities big. Run DMC were every black kids hero. Rap was becoming strong; and Donnie, like Elvis Presley (thirty years before), found his soul and began to "be down". Donnie took the positive side. He saw rap, the music, the dances, the "fresh" kids with their sneakers—their way, the black kids way, that was strong—not the negative side (the drugs, the stupidity);

and Donnie emerged into the soul and funk. He made it his thing and he was accepted.

Donnie would soon get a call from Mary Alford, a North Dorchester white girl who had managed a black soul group named Margo Thunder and Entrigue. Some months prior, Donnie had gotten a hundred dollars for his birthday and went out to buy a red leather Michael Jackson jacket, complete with sunglasses and a white glove. In fact, that summer, everything was Michael Jackson—his room was covered from ceiling to floor with Michael Jackson. Donnie had Michael Jackson buttons and would give them to any kid who would do the "moonwalk" with him….and the black kids loved him.

After he learned enough, Donnie "busted out" and jumped on a few talent shows in Roxbury and Dorchester. One of them was Maurice Starr's "Hollywood Talent Show", where in November 1981, the New Edition had been discovered by Maurice Starr. Donnie lip-sync'd and danced intensely, impersonating Michael Jackson; and got some notoriety around the black and white neighborhoods.

Donnie, having some success with his Michael Jackson routine, decided to explore rap deeper, and hooked up with his friend Danny to start a rap group. Donnie explains why he and the group were so knowledgeable about black culture. He notes, "In the first grade I was being bussed to a school in an all black area. We were all bussed to black schools, all except Joe. He didn't go to a black school, but he still knows the black culture. Contrary to what the white racists think about bussing, it was the greatest thing to happen to us. " Donnie continues, "musically, all the New Kids were influenced by black artists. Danny was a rapper just like I was. We all listened to a lot of R & B. That's what our friends were into. Singing black came natural to us."

Naturally, Donnie would be the first—with his freshness, his def sneakers, his brashness and his "Hey, I'm ready" attitude.

The Rise of New Kids on the Block...

When the call came in 1984, Donnie Wahlberg, who with his five brothers had a neighborhood "rep" as tough guys, but was better known for his Michael Jackson impersonations, was ready. He jumped up, to get down into Roxbury, and met Maurice Starr, and later that night, called Jordan, Jonathan and Danny.

Now, fate is something else! As you all might know by now! So I'm going to tell you a story—a fairy tale, if you will—a story of how fate and dreams and belief made something great happen in this world. Call it a natural phenomenon.

Chapter Two
Jordan

Jordan Nathaniel Marcel Knight was born May 17, 1970. His parents Marlene and Allen had five other children: Allison, Sharon, David, Chris and Jonathan. His mother called him her enchanted one. He was chubby and had big chubby cheeks, beautiful black hair and big dark brown eyes.

Jordan's mom is a very special person, a Canadian—English Canadian, not French Canadian. She was raised in the Episcopalian faith and, like the other New Kid's moms, her life centered around her church and God's teachings. Jordan's dad was an Episcopalian minister. Both parents were devoted to the teachings of Christ and believed in practicing Christ's teachings of love and giving and acceptance of theirs and their children's lives. Marlene explains how she named David, Jonathan and Jordan this way. "I wanted to get as many Biblical names as possible in my family. David and Jonathan are good friends in the Bible; and David is my first-born son, and Jonathan my second. Jordan, well I named him after the River Jordan. It was a name I found very attractive and it was unusual. Nathaniel, I also got from the Bible; and Marcel, well, at the time there was some political upheaval in Canada between the French and English Canadians, and I wanted to make a political statement by giving him a French name to try to connect the two sides together."

Marlene and Allen were very much in love and wanted to share that love with as many people as possible. When Jordan was born, the family lived in Worcester, a small city about fifty miles from Boston. Soon after, when Jordan was three years old, Allen Knight was named Minister of the All Saints Episcopal Church and the family moved to North Dorchester, where they lived in a ten-bedroom house. Their home was huge and Marlene and Allen filled it not only with their children, but with many foster children of all races and colors. One of those children was Christopher, a child of African descent. The Episcopal religion, like the Baptist and Catholic religions, has a strong missionary outreach program, involving people all over the world of all colors, races and creeds. It was not uncommon of people, like the Knights, who had a strong faith and belief in the basic Christian ideals of love, help, sharing and giving to not only give their time and money to stop world poverty, but to go a step further—believing that to help one person in need is to take one step toward destroying child neglect and abuse, and hunger in the world. And so, they adopted Christopher and raised him as a son, with Allison, Sharon, David, Jonathan and Jordan. Into this loving, healthy, happy family Jonathan and Jordan were born and raised.

Jordan heard music right from the beginning. Both Marlene and Allen, plus his grandparents, played piano and read music. Performing and playing music was a very natural thing in the Knight household. Jordan began singing when he was very small. He was trained in an Episcopal church boys choir, singing the treble/soprano part. All the Knights were very involved in the church choir at All Saints' Episcopal Church in Dorchester. The church, for Jordan and his family, was a place where they socialized, made friends, performed, and made a joyful noise unto the Lord with their voices. Their earliest memories are of themselves in the church choir wearing their robes, happy, smiling and singing.

At the age of three, when Jordan and his family moved to Dorchester, he went to Headstart, a pre-school program begun by the City of Boston to prepare young children earlier for public school. There were Headstart Programs in Roxbury, Dorchester and

North Dorchester. Unlike Roxbury, the Dorchester and North Dorchester Communities were racially integrated, and Jordan came in contact with the black culture early in life. During his first year at Headstart, Jordan made his first stage appearance as Baby Jesus at the Christmas Pageant. Marlene reflects, "I remember when he came onto the stage. He was dressed in all white, and he had this beautiful curly black hair and black eyes. He had a gorgeous smile and big fat cheeks. The audience went *awww*! He was so beautiful. That was the first time I saw the kid on stage."

In 1975, North Dorchester, Dorchester, Roxbury and Mattapan would be going through some very intense situations....like integration of the Boston Public Schools. Now this was not exactly true, in its finer points. Technical High, a highly rated college-preparatory school situated right in the heart of Roxbury on Warren Street had always been integrated. White students had been taking busses from all over the city to come to Technical High School in the black community for a long time. Boston Technical, Boston English and Boston Latin High all had excellent reputations for sending kids to college, and usually had the best basketball and football teams in the city. Now, Boston English and Boston Latin are located in the Fenway area of Boston across the street from one another and got the cream of the crop of black and white, Asiatic and Spanish students. During the sixties and seventies, Dorchester High in Boston, though not in the same class as Latin, English and Technical, had a very substantial black and white student population, as did Jeremiah Burke (an all girls school that became coed in the late seventies). Thus, all of the high schools in Roxbury, Dorchester and North Dorchester were already integrated.

But! There were four things that caused the Federal Government to place Judge Garrity (a Federal Judge) in control of the official integration of the Boston Public Schools. (1) The Federal Government has given the City of Boston some money. (2) Two middle schools and one high school—the Joseph Lee and the William Trotter Middle Schools and Madison Park High were built and completed in the early seventies in Roxbury and Dorchester. (3) And, there were three places in Boston where the black population did not work, live, or go to school....three places so totally segregated that their namesake schools (Charlestown High, South Boston High and Hyde Park High) up to 1975, had never had a black kid or minority kid walk through their halls. We have established that black and white kids went to high school together in Roxbury and Dorchester. But, (4) the elementary and junior high schools were totally segregated in each neighborhood. Black kids went to all black schools; and white kids went to all white schools.

In 1975, the City of Boston with Mayor Kevin White in charge, pushed by the Federal Government, with Judge Garrity in charge, went to war against racial segregation—using kids as their weapons. It was simple, but looked complicated. Here was the plan; white kids would be bussed across town to all black schools in the elementary and junior high grade levels and black kids would be bussed across town to all white high schools. Simple! Huh?

Well, all hell broke loose in Boston! The kids were bussed amongst fears of white parents that their kids would receive an inferior education, and develop drug habits; and, black parents feared the violence and the hatred that they knew existed for their children, in the white areas.

So, here's what happened. The black kids being bussed were called everything but a child of God, and the parents of the white kids in South Boston, Charlestown and Hyde Park burned buses, spat on kids, threw rocks, intimidated and humiliated the black kids from Roxbury and Dorchester. The white kids being bussed into Roxbury, Jamaica Plain, and Hyde Park were met with no resistance from the parents, because secretly they hoped that the level of teaching and education in their kids' schools would rise up because of the white integration. And, of course it did. But, inside the schools there would be some friction at first. The black kids could be hard. Most lived in projects or apartments. The white kids, although inner-city kids who knew the streets, came for the most part from homes with two parents and large families with strong neighborhood ties. So, there were some fights and some name-calling, but they learned to respect each other and get the positive things from one another's culture. For the black kids at the white schools, acceptance took longer. It was harder because the white parents made it hard. But, in the end, the kids worked it out themselves.

So, it ended like this. Those black parents who could, sent their kids to M.E.T.C.O., an organization that was begun in 1966 by Ellen Jackson in Roxbury. This organization bussed black kids in huge numbers to the best white schools, such as Lexington High, Concord-Carlisle High, Belmont High and Newton-Wellesley High. These schools were located in wealthy suburban towns and this program was, and is today, hugely successful. The white parents who could afford it took their kids out of South Boston High, Charlestown High and Hyde Park High, and sent them to parochial and private schools, as did some parents in North Dorchester and Jamaica Plain. Gradually, South Boston High and Hyde Park High would become predominantly black.

So, by the time Donnie, Danny, Jordan and Jonathan entered this turmoiled school system, here's what was left; Real poor kids with no where else to go; people (adults and kids alike) who wanted to make the schools work; and, people who felt they had something to learn from one another and wanted peace between the races.

The Episcopalian Church to which the Knight family belongs, has always had a liberal attitude. Its churches are very well integrated. In fact, Jordan's brother Chris was an acolyte, an assistant in the church and the leader of the Episcopalian Church in America was a black woman. Thus, Marlene and Allen Knight saw no problem in busing their children across town to Roxbury.

The Roman Catholic Church and St. Elizabeth's Parish where Donnie's mother Alma gave fundraisers and danced in musicals, was not integrated at all. In fact, very few Catholic Parishes had a mix of black and white worshipers. But the Knights were Episcopalian and from Dorchester; and they weren't poor (but they weren't rich either) and they weren't running. They would stick it out and their kids would go to school across town in Roxbury. Besides, there were sufficient numbers of them and they could take care of themselves.

Thus, the first stage was set. The dream would begin. Destiny and fate took over. Donnie, Danny, Jonathan and Jordan would go to school with black kids. Oh yeah! Because he had this big musical side to him, Jordan would always be in the church choir and he would receive additional voice training at the Royal School of Church Music Summer Camp at Princeton University. Christmas's would be spent at his grandmother's house in Ontario.

But, at school he learned about break-dancing; and that became his claim to fame in the black and white neighborhoods. As Marlene said, "He loved to breakdance. Even before break dancing was a craze in Boston, Jordan was with a youth organization near our home. They put on breakdancing shows and demonstrations and taught kids how to breakdance. Most of his time after school was spent with that youth organization breakdancing. He even did some touring around different states breakdancing with that group." Jordan loved drawing graffiti. He would spend hours in his bedroom drawing pictures and writing. But, it was the performing that turned him on—breakdancing for a crowd and performing regularly with the church choir.

So, when Donnie called Jordan, he knew Roxbury well, and he was ready to go down and see Maurice. "And besides", said Donnie, "that's the guy who discovered the New Edition!"

The Rise of New Kids on the Block...

Chapter Three
Jonathan

Jonathan Rashleigh Knight a Sagittarian, was born November 29, 1968. His parents Marlene and Allen Knight had five other children—Allison Sharon, David, Chris (who was adopted before Jonathan was born) and Jordan. Marlene and Allen Knight were very well educated. Marlene had a degree in physiology and Allen was an ordained Episcopalian minister.

Both Jonathan and Jordan inherited their good looks from their parents. Their mother Marlene was a beautiful English Canadian who gave her children their gorgeous black hair and big dark eyes. Every summer the family would go to their grandparents' cottage in Ontario and spend lots of time at the beach. They were a peaceful, proud and dignified family.

The universe is huge, and we live but a millisecond. We are blinks of light on the earth and always the hand of God sets the course; and Marlene, perhaps seeing something no one else could understand, named her three biological sons after a prince, a king of Israel and a river.

(Samuel 18:1) "And it came to pass, when he had made an end of speaking unto Saul, That the soul of Jonathan was knit with the soul of David, and Jonathan loved him as his own."

Marlene would have known this verse, when she named David and Jonathan. Jonathan, the protector, as he now protects the New Kids

The Rise of New Kids on the Block...

on the Block, the perpetual "big brother" and Jordan her enchanted son, Marlene named for the River Jordan.

(Matthew 3:13) "Then cometh Jesus from Galilee to the River Jordan unto John the Baptist, to be baptized by him." And Marlene would be well pleased with her sons. Jonathan was very quiet as a child. He won an award for writing a Christmas story about Santa Claus. He liked to, as a child and even now, talk about people, events and situations. Jonathan was a friendly outgoing baby and, as he grew, he became even more sociable. He would whisper in people's ears telling them secrets and stories. He was very creative and sweet.

Jonathan Rashleigh Knight—Rashleigh was a maiden name of his father's mother, a name that goes back many generations in his family—loved going to church, the music, the secular surrounding and the singing. He enjoyed watching his brothers and sisters singing, hearing his own voice soaring to the heavens (the choir was his favorite place).

Growing up in North Dorchester, living in the square (Ashmont Station Region) was very different for Jonathan, who was four when his family moved from Worcester. Donnie's and Danny's families were old hat to the region. North Dorchester was their stomping grounds. But, for the Knights, with their large and always extending family, Boston was huge and different. Nearby was the Dorchester Court House where the roughest white, and mainly black thugs, went to hear if they got off or not (meaning did they go home, or to Charles Street Jail). A few of Donnie's brothers would make that trip from time to time; but Jonathan's family had All-Saint's Episcopal Church music all day and all night. There was always music—always somebody playing the piano, and singing constantly. There were plenty of kids running around their 17-room, 4-bedroom house. Their home was shared by dozens of foster kids and adults through the years and Jonathan and Jordan learned to get along with all kinds of people.

There was, to be sure, a difference in living inner-city life, but Jonathan got along and learned the streets well. But he never let the streets eat him up. He and the other New Kids watched as kids on both sides (black and white) began to go deeper and deeper into drugs. Yet, Jonathan, Jordan, Donnie and Danny who had known each other from kindergarten up to the seventh grade, and found each other again through Donnie in high school, would remain drug-free in the company of themselves and other kids like themselves.

Four of the New Kids lived in an area bordered by five main streets—Washington Street/Talbot Avenue/Ashmont Street/ Dorchester Avenue/Columbia Road. It looks something like this:

> Washington Street, between Codman Square and Columbia Road was the border between black and white. One side of Washington Street was called Dorchester (black), the other side was called North Dorchester (white). Now everybody knew that if you were walking up Washington Street towards Codman Square, and you took a left at "Let's say the Dorchester Court House" you would be in

white territory; and probably nothing would happen unless you were black and you walked too far—let's say, down to Dorchester Avenue—and kept going, and it was real late at night. And, everybody knew that, if you walked up to the courthouse from Melbourne Street to Washington Street, and crossed over from Washington Street to the other side, and stood on the sidewalk and you were white; then you either were crazy, or you had escaped from the Dorchester Court House jail. Thus, you were a bad cat, and definitely not to be messed with.

But, Jonathan and the New Kids got along well with everybody, Donnie and Danny, with their soulfulness and funky respect of black culture, mixed with Jordan's angelicness and Jonathan's studied honest cool, earned them respect. And, at age 15 and 16, they were taking the bus to Dudley Station, traveling to Maurice Starr's house in Roxbury. During Jonathan's years growing up, he would sing with Jordan in the church choir; and with Jordan and Danny in their school choir. But not Donnie! Donne was into rap and dancing; and wouldn't sing until Maurice told him he could, and showed him how.

Dedicated, Jonathan would put all his energy into singing. Girls for both brothers would come later. For Jonathan, his first crush would be when he was eight. But like all of the New Kids, they were friends with girls. There wasn't a lot of dating. Jonathan had some close girlfriends from school, and they all had some crushes on girls, but nothing heavy. They were good kids, who could wait, and they had a lot of respect for girls and their feelings. But mainly, they were into their music, singing and dancing; and this was before Cheese would call J. Jizzon and Puff McCloud telling them about this black guy in Roxbury, who wanted to start a singing group with white kids. Before long, they would have millions of adoring girlfriends all over the world.

Chapter Four
Danny

Daniel William Wood, Jr., a Taurus, was born May 14, 1970. His parents Elizabeth and Daniel had five other children—Bethany, Melissa, Pam, Brett and Rachel. Elizabeth, a no-nonsense petite, dark-haired Roman Catholic, believed in raising children normally and properly. Daniel, a hard working community man, with a rough edge believed in family togetherness, with lots of love and respect for one another. Into this strict North Dorchester family, Danny came home. And what a home it was! A big old Dorchester Victorian house filled with three beautiful girls ready to throw all their love to this dark-haired big brown-eyed baby boy.

This was the first boy for Elizabeth and Daniel. They had three girls, in as many years, hoping each time that this one would be the boy. They tried again, and 1970 proved to be the lucky year. Daniel, Sr., beamed with pride and joy, and gave his first-born son his name, Daniel.

Danny was a delightful baby, very energetic, his big eyes going from Bethany to Melissa, to Pam as they hovered over his crib, picking him up, marveling at his every move, laughing and tickling him. Little Danny never became spoiled. All that love made him want to make them as proud of him as he could. So, he'd toddle after his sisters, grinning while they heaped praise and love all over him. Danny learned how to love and respect girls very early in life. When Danny was born, his sisters were 3, 4, and 5, and he remembers those years spent with them as his happiest years.

Like all the New Kids, Danny grew up safe and secure, in the bosom of a large family where love, respect, giving and sharing were the main things in life. Danny's most prized possessions were a teddy bear and teddy bear puppet, that Elizabeth and Daniel gave him when he was a toddler. Danny, who would become the most athletic and quick-tempered of the New Kids, showed, at an early age, the kind of sensitivity that only a real boy could have. Danny kept those bears his whole life; and when you went to his house, you could hold them, touch them, and work the puppet.

Danny's life was tempered with death. As a kid, two of his cousins who were the same age as him, lost their father, and Danny watched his family being buried—his uncle, an aunt, and a cousin, and while on tour as a New Kid, he lost his grandfather. These deaths were real hard for him to deal with, and probably accounted for his far away gaze, at times. But, Danny would channel these grievances into an athletic prowess. He had great physical control over his muscles, and could get them to do what he wanted them to. Danny's energetic spirit wanted the fast track.

At seven, Danny joined a track club and became a runner, but not just a runner—Danny would compete and win numerous track trophies. He was an excellent runner, a very good athlete. Running gave Danny great discipline and, not only razor sharpened his body, but strengthened his mind giving him a quick agile way of walking and talking. A runner's discipline is different from that of any other sport except boxing or tennis. A runner is alone and has to learn how to set his pace. A runner sizes up opponents, based on their individual talents. A runner doesn't back down for anything, and a runner will take a while to analytically make a decision. When Donnie called Danny, Danny could take his time, seeing if it was right for him and if he was right for it. Being an athlete, having the confidence that comes from knowing your body and mind on a higher level, Danny could wait. But as we all know, Donnie is a good talker and helped Danny make the "right" decision.

In elementary school, Danny joined a swing chorus, where he could exercise another of his talents. Always wanting to make his family proud of him, Danny stuck with it and toured all over the city of Boston, giving performances with, whom Danny says, was the finest musical director in the city. Danny enjoyed being in the chorus. Like the other New Kids, because of his performances around the city (especially while competing with other track clubs) Danny came in contact, in a very positive way, with black kids from Roxbury and Dorchester.

Donnie and Danny were a twosome; like Jordan and Jonathan were a twosome. All the New Kids knew one another; but Donnie and Danny "hung tough". In fact, Donnie probably called Danny, after auditioning for Maurice Starr; and Mary Alford had dropped him at home. But Danny, knowing Donnie's strong talent for stretching realism, probably said, "Aw what are you talking about?" Danny laid back; so, Donnie called Jordan and Jonathan; and this time, Donnie would be on target, because he had met (in musical terms) "The Real Thing".

Yeah! Donnie and Danny were best friends; and Donnie, being into dancing, music and rap; noticing his left-handed friend's athletic ability, convinced him that they could rap and dance together. So, they spent many hours, after school, putting together some raps with a few dance steps—stuff they were picking up from the black guys at school. and, when Danny saw some kids break-dancing, he fell in love with the black culture and became a rapper/break-dancer (besides, he had messed up his knee and couldn't compete at track anymore). So, using this as his outlet for athletics—break-dancing, where you had to use every muscle in your body; break-dancing, where you have to have control of every muscle God gave you; break-dancing, where you could compete with other break-dancers and win! O, yeah! Danny became a break-dancer, like Jordan, and Donnie was a rapper and Jonathan could sing, baby! And, here comes fate, coming on strong!

And, the positive black culture was in these boys from North Dorchester, when the next call from Cheese came. Puff McLoud was a break-dancer! A rapper! And a member of a group called "Rock Against Racism"!

Chapter Five
Joey

Joseph Mulrey McIntyre, a Capricorn, was born December 31, 1972. His parents Thomas and Kay McIntyre had eight other children—Judith, Alice, Susan, Patricia, Carol, Jean, Kate and Tommy.

Christmas Day 1972 was like every other Christmas in the huge Irish-American Catholic McIntyre family. The day was noisy and loud, and the air was filled with the excitement only happy girls, squealing with joy and enough presents to fill a toy store could make, and a young boy who would, up until a week from that Christmas Day, be Tom and Kay's only male child. The oldest girls—Judy, Alice and Susan, were teenagers who brought presents for their younger sisters, brother and parents, and with their parents buying presents for everyone, plus the younger siblings (Patricia, Carol, Jean, Kate and young Tom) chipping in. With an average of four presents a person, there would be loads of presents in the McIntyre house, plus enough food to feed a small army.

This Christmas (1972), when all the McIntyre clan would be under one roof in their spacious Needham, Massachusetts home, after all the gift wrapped presents had been ripped and torn open—producing dolls, carriages, doll houses, new bicycles, games and clothes; and after all the food and desert had been sent to the stomachs of some very happy and exhausted kids, Mrs. McIntyre had one more present—one more surprise for all of them. This gift had been given nine years before, on the same date, to Judy, Alice, Susan, Patricia and her husband Tom, in the form of a lovely baby daughter named

Carol. Now, this gift from God would again be given to the entire McIntyre family.

One week after Mrs. McIntyre and her large, beautiful family returned from Christmas Mass, McIntyre family history repeated itself; and, on New Year's Day, 1972, Joseph Mulrey McIntyre came into the world, with outrageously large, round, blue eyes and a tiny bow-shaped mouth. He was gorgeous, absolutely beautiful! But, some of the girls thought he looked like a chicken when he first came home from the hospital, and as his big sister Judy says, "Can you imagine anyone saying that about Joseph McIntyre today?"

Joseph was going to be called Christopher. From the day his mother conceived him, he was Christopher in her mind. But, his father Thomas, a robust Irishman, a brick-layer, who would later become the president of the Boston Bricklayers' Union, had a very good friend—a family friend, who the McIntyres considered a member of their own immediate family. His name was Joseph, and on December 31, 1972—the day Kay entered the hospital to give birth—her thoughts were of Joseph who had befriended her husband in a special way. And, she knew the great respect and admiration these two men had for each other. So Christopher became Joseph, and the family name Mulrey was given to him as a keepsake.

Donnie has said that the New Kids were put together by fate, and as Maurice Starr would say, "Fate is God's work." Thus, it would be Donnie who would call three friends of his, blessed with Biblical names. Daniel was a prophet of God—a man of great understanding and visions—whose wisdom and thought and counsel was blessed by God. He was a prince, under the reigns of Neb-u-chad-nez-zar of Babylon and Darius and Cyrus, kings of Persia.

Jonathan was a prince of Judea, son of the first king of Israel, and good friend to David, a king of Israel, and Judea, from whom the saviour of the world, Jesus Christ's lineage was traced; and Jordan, who's river Christ was baptized in. And, Maurice Starr would discover Joseph, a name synonymous with Joseph (earthly father of

Jesus Christ)—a man who would raise the Christ Child; save his life by fleeing to Egypt during Herod's massacre of all babies under two years of age; and, who taught "Our Lord" the trade of carpentry and building. Two thousand years later, a builder and bricklayer named Thomas, would name his second son after his friend Joseph—a guilder, mason, bricklayer, and carpenter.

Joseph Mulrey McIntrye was born into a tightknit talented family who's acting, dancing, singing and musical talents were legendary in their Massachusetts communities of Needham and Jamaica Plain. Joseph's grandfather, on Kay's side of the family, earned his way through Boston College singing and playing piano, and not just playing the piano, Kay reminisces: "He made the piano talk; he had the softest touch; everyone loved my dad. I think back now of getting up at the supper table and going into the living room. My sister would be sitting there. I would be sitting in the big chair, and my father would play for us. If we only had tape recorders then! I could hear my father play again…."

Joseph's mother Kay, an aristocratic-looking Irish woman, grew up in a home filled with music, singing and laughter. Even after marrying Thomas and making a decision to have and raise a large family. Kay never let her dreams of acting and singing on stage stop her. As each child was born, Kay would direct them in acting and song, making herself and her growing brood a community treasure. They would put on little neighborhood shows and perform for relatives and adults that came to visit. This would continue until they moved to Jamaica Plain in Boston, where Kay joined America's oldest community theatre the Footlight Club (established one hundred and fifteen years before on Elliot Street in the Jamaica Plain section of Boston). Kay would work and act at the theater for twenty years, bringing her children one by one into the sawdust and costume world of showbusiness.

Kay was terrific, and both parents encouraged their children's talents at performing. Joseph says "Even before I joined New Kids, my family had always been pretty well-known around my neighborhood. We'd have a great time at holidays; not only would we do serious performing in front of our relatives, but we'd goof around too. For instance, we'd pull out our tennis rackets and make believe they were guitars, while we jumped around and pretended to be rock stars. Those were the days!"

From the very beginning, as a toddler, Joseph displayed signs of inherent talent. All the relatives and adults had to say was "Joe, sing such and such", and Joe would get right up and sing; and know all the words. But, in Kay's mind, all were equally talented, and she pushed her seven daughters and two sons to excel on stage. Before long, the singing and dancing McIntyres would perform separately, and together at the Footlight Club. Kay would walk Joseph and the other kids to school, and after school, Joe began to go to the Footlight Club where his mother worked. He would go to rehearsals and watch very closely. Everyone knew Joe. They knew him from the Footlight Club and the Neighborhood Children's Theater.

The church, as in all of the New Kids' families, was very important to their lives, and at church Joseph would begin his professional career. The Neighborhood Children's Theater was begun for the church by a very talented young woman. At the age of six Joe became active in the church theater group, singing and acting. His sister Carol joined too, and Joe would perform the title role in Oliver, and she would play Nancy. Joe was also the little boy in "The Music Man". His mother remembers, "You never had to say anything to him. He was just very laid back about it. He would do his bit, stop the show, and go home. He never made a big thing about it". Joseph loved the stage, he loved the theater, and he was a good kid.

They would raise money and go on trips too. The theatre group would perform in red tee shirts with their names on the front, worn with dungarees and white turtleneck shirts. Joe and his sister Carol were among the first thirteen to join the little theatre group that grew to sixty kids. The group canvassed the neighborhood, raising money to go on tour; and they performed in places like New York, Washington, D.C. and Florida. At six, Joe was a professional actor. One of Joe's favorite memories is of a play in Jamaica Plain at the Footlight Club where his sisters, brother, mother and he were singing and acting on stage. Recalls Joe, "My dad was sitting in the back row of the auditorium, and he was very proud to see us all up there together. It was great!"

Although acting held a high place in the McIntyre family, education came first. Joseph worked hard. He was going to rehearsals at night while attending grammar school. At Catholic Memorial, as a freshman, he received first honors and received an academic award. The perfect student, Joseph loved doing homework and had a great time at school. But, sometimes girls were on his mind. Joe tells how he got his first kiss at a Christmas party when he was eleven years old. It was in an attic. The lights went out as she was coming up the stairs. "I saw her shadow, and knew it was her. Everyone was just going crazy because the lights were out, so I just started kissing her. It was nice."

The super close McIntyre family deeply encouraged one another towards their goals. Whatever one did, was accepted by all, and the family excelled dynamically. Judy, Joe's big sister, called by Kay "the finest actress she had ever seen", went to New York where she acted on both the New York stage and television, including the "Guiding Light" and two other soap operas. Judith remembers Joe as being equally skilled at both singing and acting, with singing being his first choice. She tells a story of how when Joe and herself played sister and brother at the Footlight Club Community Theater Production of "Our Town", Joe thought that it was his biggest acting challenge, because in the third act he had to sit in a chair for half an hour as a dead person and not move.

To be destined for anything in life, some would say that it's a supernatural thing. Some people would also say that to have a gift or talent from God, well that's all you need to be successful. But, from the time you are born, there are people and events that can influence your life, and if most of them are positive then your life will be shaped accordingly. Such was the case with Tom and Kay in raising Joseph and his many sisters and brother. Tom and Kay were very strict disciplinarians. They were Roman Catholics and there were rules and regulations that had to be followed. Mass was a prerequisite and the entire family could be seen every Sunday at church. The children had to be in at certain times, behave very well in school, dress properly, be well-mannered and respect people of all races, creeds and religions. The biggest influence for Joseph and the large McIntyre clan was Thomas and Kay McIntyre, their parents. Thomas, a strong-willed, fair-minded man gave every consideration to his growing family, loving each one equally and devotedly. Although, not a participant in their community theatre projects, he was their biggest supporter. As a bricklayer in Boston he worked with a variety of men—blacks from Roxbury, Italians from the North End, Jews from Brookline. To him, they were all just men getting a job done and feeding their families.

Joey

At home, there would be no racial talk, no prejudicial talk around the dinner table where every McIntyre was expected to eat together as long as they lived at home. Oh! It could be brutal around the table! Irish humor can be filled with sarcasm, as was the McIntyre's because there were so many of them, each with their own brand of independence and strength. That humor, teasing and ribbing one another, was essential to McIntyre life; and Joseph, being the youngest, listened to all the jokes, singing, and laughter coming from his family, assimilating every bit of it, so that when he joined Donnie, Danny, Jordan and Jonathan (all of whom themselves came from big families), well, little Joseph (at twelve years old) could take whatever they dished out to him and give it right back. And, the most important thing was that around the dinner table, and in the world itself, Tom and Kay McIntyre, by their own example, did not allow the ignorance of racial prejudice to creep into theirs or their children's lives.

They were not the Kennedy type (Irish rich, with great political backgrounds and futures ahead of them), nor were they the South Boston type of Irish (clannish and not interested in other people's cultures). No! The McIntyres were aristocratic, artistic, hard-working people whose enjoyment of life spilled over into bowling, singing, dancing, acting, and being good to all people. And, Joseph watched his parents leading him, by their example.

Well, when Mary Alford called in June of 1985, and asked if they would bring Joseph to Roxbury to audition for a record producer named Maurice Starr, to be a part of a group of kids that Maurice Starr was hoping to record, the McIntyres took this request as seriously as they would have if a producer on Broadway had asked to audition Joseph, and arranged a date. Mary Alford drove twelve year old Joe from his home on Elliot Street to 27 Dudley Street in Roxbury, where Maurice Starr, a big hulking man of thirty years had just bought a house for $27,500.00. (Ironically, at that very moment, Maurice was going through a legal battle with the New Edition, that would keep him in court until November 1987).

The Rise of New Kids on the Block...

At the audition, Joey sang sweetly. Maurice, noting that he had an operatic voice, got Joey a Michael Jackson album and told him to listen to the way Michael handles his phrases—the way he uses the vibrato. Maurice, then, nodded his head at Mary, giving her the high five sign. On their way back to Joe's house, Mary told little twelve year old Joey that he had the job, if he wanted it! Luckily, Joey McIntyre said, "Yes!"

Part Two
Maurice Starr

The Rise of New Kids on the Block...

Chapter Six
The Johnson Family Foundation

Maurice Starr, a Scorpio, was born Lawrence "Larry" Johnson, November 19th, 1953. His parents Ray, Senior and Willie Mae Johnson had six children, Elvin, Ray Junior, Donald, Calvin, Larry and Michael.

When Larry took his first steps as a toddler, his father placed him beside his mother on the piano bench so that Larry would hear the soft tones and melodic notes his mother would play, and he could watch her hands glide effortlessly over the piano keys. As each child was born (from the oldest Elvin to the baby Michael), this scenario would be repeated again and again. As each child grew older, Ray and Willie Mae would start talking in another language—a language of A# and B flat, major and minor keys, of chords and modulations, of key changes and rhythm playing, of scales and dominant scales; and they would play horns and piano. Ray would play some guitar, and they would play for the children and show them how to hold their instruments, how to hear their instruments, how the instrument (the music it made) and you became as one. And, as each child grew older, and before each child could walk, Ray and Willie Mae's child could carry a note, sing and hum a few bars and play some chorus on the piano perfectly.

By the time Elvin was seven, and the baddest cat alive (outside of Ma and Daddy), he was the best musician in the family, as all of the brothers would say over and over many years later. Ray, at six and Donnie, at four, were coming along, getting that music theory down, and Calvin, at three, was grooving to the way Daddy played trumpet. He knew how to finger it, how to wrap his little baby hands around it, how to blow sweetly and softly and get his sound from the trumpet. At the same time, little Larry was crawling up to the piano so that he could get his taste, so he could see what it was all about, so he could hear, for himself, Mama's sweet soul playing, and, Larry knew forever (right then and there) that he would do nothing else (nothing else, man) but hear those sweet melodic sounds in his head—always, and play them forever—always. And, baby brother Michael would hear the groove from his mother's stomach.

Down South in the twenties, thirties, forties, fifties. Hey! Down South, at any time in American history, was rough on people of African descent. For African-Americans, called Negroes or colored (or worse), life could be one degrading step after another. Most lived in segregated communities, and like any community, anywhere, there were the good people and the bad people; and unlike any other communities, anywhere else in America, the Southern and Midwest communities had the great music people.

O, Yeah! Tell me about it! Louis Armstrong, Charlie "Bird" Parker, Charlie Christian, Miles Davis, John Coltrane, Thelonius Sphere Monk, Duke Ellington, Art Blakeley, Rashan Roland Kirk, Ahmad Jamal, Ray Charles, Ella Fitzgerald, Dinah Washington, Dizzie Gillespie, Juion Cook, Elvin Jones, Billie Holiday, Sarah Vaughan, Nat King Cole, Billie Eckstine, B.B King, Muddy Waters, Earl "Fatha" Hines and Huddie Ledbetter ("Leadbelly"). O, man! And there's more! The Mills Brothers, Ink Spots, Jackie McLean, Charles Mingus, Cab Calloway, Max Roach, Bessie Smith, Art Tatum, Lester Young, Lionel Hampton, Count Basie, Bind Lemon Jefferson and Ma Rainey. Man! Millions of known greats and unsung heroes moving through the colored communities in the twenties, thirties, forties and fifties.

They played at night and slept during the day, playing that chittling circuit, the juke joints, the chicken shacks, the bars and the lounges. Hey! They were playing at night-time, 'cause it's the right-time; playing hard and living fast, playing for the people, making life a little easy…making life a little less hard for the people, and all the while thinking "Not making no money now, but I got my taste and I got my sweet thing, and I got my people"….Kansas City, New Orleans, The Savoy, Birdland, Chicago.

That first Charlie "Bird" Parker Quintet featured Bird on saxophone, Miles Davis on trumpet, Max Roach on drums, Duke Jordan on piano, and Tommy Porter on bass. These real deal players—these jazz men, blues men, bebop men, rhythm and blues men, hootchie coochie men, uptown men—these men played for their lives until they became discovered. Some became visible to the white eye. The Caucasian European eye sees this "new thing", hears these new rhythms—and now, the colored secret is out. "These cats are bad!"

New York, Chicago here I come!" Doors opened at Dial Records, Savoy Records, Chess Records, Mercury Records, Columbia Records (the House Bessie Smith built when she sang "Gimme a Pigfoot and a Bottle of Beer"), Spotlight Records, Coral Records and Metro Records. After playing live before thousands in their own black communities, paying those heavy dues, now they could record and the records would come out, get some…hell…a lot of radio play, and millions of people would hear them; and white dudes would copy them, make some money; and the colored would pay some more heavy, heavy dues.

Brother Ray, in the thirties and forties, was one of them—a journeyman musician who played with plenty of respect from the other cats. He was traveling, playing and recording with the great Lionel Hampton Orchestra and the Count Basie Band, as well as hundreds of pick-up gigs throughout the South. Ray's musical theory was impeccable, and he could play five instruments proficiently and by playing with some well-known bands, he learned early, the recording end of music...the recording studio environment.

Ray was a jazzman and could stomp the blues into the ground down and dirty and he was also a God-fearing Southern man, raised in the moral and spiritual roots of Jesus Christ. He believed that alcohol, tobacco and drugs did not have a place in his life and that all a musician needed was his talent to live by. Thus, when Ray met Willie Mae (a fine young pianist and singer who had done some gigging and was also a featured artist at some points with the Count Basie Band and the Lionel Hampton Orchestra), they fell in love, got married and decided to begin raising a family right away. Ray, not fighting love—unlike some of his contemporaries—and not being hooked on that needle and alcohol, made his choice (the right choice for him) to cut down on his traveling. He settled down, but continued to see old friends, like B.B. King and Lionel Hampton; and hit the road, sometimes (if he needed the money or he had "the feeling"). But for the most part, Ray and Willie Mae's life centered around their growing family, spreading their musical talents to their children.

And, before you could say "one, two, three, four, five, six, seven, eight" the Johnson's had become a family band, playing at churches, social dances, clubs and talent shows. They were everywhere in Deland, Florida; building a name and gaining fame. Larry Johnson's early life in Deland, Florida, is remarkable. Deland, situated in Central Florida, smack-dab between Daytona Beach and Orlando or fifteen minutes from Daytona Beach, and a half-hour from Disneyland, was also only fifteen miles from Interstate 95, which, for a traveling musician like Ray, meant easy access to big cities, north and south. Orlando and Daytona Beach were alien planets to Larry. Traveling to these places and seeing these sights would have been like getting in the space shuttle and going to Mars to check out the sights. By 1967-68 when Disney turned his sights on Orlando and made real estate property for two hundred miles around go sky high. Well, Larry and his family would have known about that, but they were Negroes and would not be a part of Disney's grand scheme. So, when in 1988-89 Maurice came home to Orlando, for the first of many dates, with the New Kids on the Block at Disney World, well, it was a personal triumph—another wall knocked down.

Yes, growing up down South was never easy. There were too many rules and regulations. If you were colored, there was the bus thing, or the bathroom thing, or the water thing, or the restaurant thing, or the store thing, or the movie thing, or the no peeking at white girls thing, although white guys could and would peek at the colored girls and, more often than not, try to do a little bit more than peeking. All this meant segregation, with the colored being segregated against, meaning, low or no jobs; bad or worse housing, emotional and physical abuse, and all the colored being hoarded, like cattle, into one corner of the city or town called, by all, "The Other Side of the Tracks", "Shanty Town", or worse.

Now, the other side of the tracks was not an unhappy place to be. You had your family, your church, your own eating places, your own funeral places, your own night spots, your own people, divided up into three factions—the good Negroes, the bad Negroes and the black entrepreneurs.

The good people went to church and had to go outside to the other side of town where they worked some kind of low-paying job for white people. This meant the lowest and most menial work. All were expected to enter by the back door, tip their hats saying "yes 'm and no 'm or yes sir, no sir all day long, never speaking unless spoken to, never looking you in the eye, and, even the most illiterate person could read a "For Whites Only" sign.

Now, segregation didn't mean separate, but equal. Oh hell no! Segregation and Economics went hand in hand. In Downtown Deland and the surrounding communities, when the colored who had to come to work in these communities (because there was no money on "the other side of town") wanted to use the bathroom, there would be two bathrooms—one white and clean, with lots of toilets to use, and one colored, usually dirty, and used by both men and women. For a woman or man who worked in a white home, they were expected to go to the bathroom or to get a drink of water outside. Economically, it worked this way, out of a city budget that would include 100% for education, buildings, road repair, city services, etc., the "other side of town" might get 10%, thus there were not enough books for education, not enough teachers, no jobs, no office buildings, and no roads on "the other side of town".'

The "bad people" didn't go anywhere near the white side of town, preferring to stay on "the other side of town" in the nightspots, on the corners, collecting some sort of welfare—anything, not to have to go over to the white side of town and be subjected to that madness, that abomination of hate, stripping you of all your dignity. No, the "bad people" would stay away, far away from those people, and at least have a little dignity under their own rules and regulations. These people usually worked jobs like prostitution, pimping, numbers, gambling, robbery—the usual vices. Their main job, though, was undermining the city government, keeping it busy, spending money and time foolishly.

Now, there were the colored entrepreneurs. These people usually found a trade or had a business on the "other side of the tracks"—the colored community. Sometimes they were family businesses: funeral services, construction and restaurants. Often, one man would decide to just start a business and hope the colored community could support it. Most often, it couldn't and the business would fold. Sometimes it could and it would be passed down in the family. But, the crème de la crème of the black community were its entertainers—musicians, singers, shouters, gospel, blues—the players. These people made colored people's lives bearable. Into this sect, would Larry Johnson and his brothers be born. Proud, dignified, church-going people who knew how to build their own homes, the value of real estate and who knew a lot about business and family togetherness.

Larry and his brothers, through the guidance of Willie Mae and Ray Sr., grew up not only knowing how to play music, but they learned how to make a dollar. Willie Mae's family, the Rayfords were known in the construction trade and had a small business. Larry and his brothers learned electrical wiring, electronics, carpentry, how to gut and rebuild a house, plumbing and how to buy and sell real estate. They were taught that ownership of land and property made you dependent on no other man.

Thus, the Johnsons and the Rayfords had very little to do with the white side of town. They owned their own property and traded and flourished, using their skills as tradesmen to help their side of town. And, as the brothers grew up, Ray, Sr., decided to devote all his time to his young and growing family, turning down a job with the Lionel Hampton Band. Instead, he got into the building trade with Willie Mae's bothers while putting together the tightest band ever seen in this country…the Johnson Brothers.

Ray, Sr., a tall, raw-boned, handsome Southern gentleman and Willie Mae, a beautiful, soft and determined woman, believed that faith in God and the family were the most essential things on this earth. Each Sunday would find the Johnsons and their growing brood in church giving thanks to the Lord for each and every blessing that came their way. At home, Ray and Willie Mae would instruct each child in the dynamics of music theory; and each child was expected to teach the youngest under him. Thus, Elvin taught Ray, Jr., and Ray, Jr. taught Donnie, and Donnie taught Calvin, and Calvin taught Larry, and Larry taught Michael. Little Michael didn't have anybody to teach; so, he developed a strong attachment to Larry, making him his protector and guide through the music world—an attachment that would last forever.

Ray, Sr. and Willie Mae taught the boys how to form a cohesive unit of playing musicians, to listen to the music, and how important eye, hand, head and mental contact was to a playing unit. Larry's parents also taught them to always care about one another—that the strongest one helped the weakest one, that if one made it, they all made it;

The Rise of New Kids on the Block...

and if one was being successful, that they all pitch in and help (doing whatever was necessary to keep that person successful. The boys never forgot this advice, and in later years, when they would attempt to do solo projects—sometimes failing, sometimes almost succeeding—there would always be a refuge within the family confines, 'cause Willie Mae made them boys (no matter who's ego was bigger or who's success was larger) stick together. They were, after all, blood; and nothing came between family.

Ray, Sr. was a jazz and rhythm and blues man. He played a guitar as good as he could play a trumpet, and he could hit 'em all if he had to. Now, Ray, Sr. had retired a little from the music scene, but that didn't mean that some of the guys didn't come to visit and play a little with the family. Little Larry and his brother would watch their parents jammin' with people like B.B. King and Lionel Hampton, and, when they weren't playing, they were listening to music by Ruth Brown, the Coasters, the Platters, Elvis and all the "greats".

At five, in 1958, Larry performed publicly for the first time as a singer. He began entering talent shows; and, at the age of eight, he won his first show by playing piano. The Growler-Deland High School Newspaper made note "Larry Johnson won the talent show competition by playing the piano." The Annual Deland High School Keyette Talent Show was held Wednesday night in the high school auditorium....the significance of high schools and talent shows Larry learned early, and would put them to extraordinary use in later years. Ray and Willie Mae had a secret they showed the boys. It went like this. "You got a show coming up, and you got to play all the hits 'cause that's what people want to hear; and since you don't have any hits, well, you got to put somebody else's hit on the record-player and learn the song, get the beat and the chords down and mimic their voice." Well, the boys did this month after month, year after year. They had it down to a science. Those boys would learn and play a new song in less than an hour, with Larry being the most adept at getting chords and arrangements out faster and better than his other brothers.

Chapter Seven
The Genius Emerges

Larry was born in 1953, the year Chuck Berry, Little Richard, Fats Domino, Bo Diddley and Screamin' Jay Hawkins broke out. By 1956, with Elvis Presley leading the way, the "new sound' was causing catastrophic screams to issue from the throats of young girls, and the guys were cool—"rebels without a cause".

By 1958, when Larry was five and could play guitar, piano, some horn and sing, and American Bandstand was "IT!" and Rock and Roll was here to stay, he knew this was it! There was nothing else, there would never be nothing else but the music. Besides, Little Richard drove him crazy. So Larry did everything mom and dad told him to, and passed it down to Michael. By the time he was eight, Larry could take the great songs right off the radio, learn them, sing them, and know every note backwards and forwards. Larry was learning, playing and singing music in the fifties. Imagine a little kid down South who had his own band and "cats" he lived with to groove with every day; and brother Elvin, at fifteen, was killing them with the way he played music. Oh, man! Can you hear the laughter and love and the music in the Johnson family home—them "cats" listening to the radio and getting real tight?

And for Larry, there was something else. He learned that, after you learned the song and made up an arrangement, and learned the lyrics, and started playing and singing it, well, you could maybe fool around a little, sing some different lyrics, change the bass line around and change a couple of chords on the piano (that was fun).

Something new. "Tutti Fruitti" became "Hootie Tootie", "Hound Dog" became "Ground Hog", and Larry laughed and said, "Hey Michael, look at this"; and he showed the new trick to Mike, and daddy said, "Hey boy you wrote a song!"...and the world opened up for Larry. A creative energy emerged larger than life, enveloping Larry's whole existence. He began listening to every song, every type of song, any song.... learning it, playing, and then doing his trick, taking that song and making it his own. He would become the best in the world at rearranging a hit song and making it a hit of his own. At nine, Larry wrote a song called "Girl in Yellow". At ten, Larry went with daddy, B.B. King and Lionel Hampton to a four-track studio in Orange City, about five miles from Deland. Now Larry, Mike and the rest of the brothers, and Willie Mae were used to going to the studio with dad. Ray, Sr. had been recording with groups for a long time, and he was in big demand as a session player. But, this day was to be something different.

Right after daddy laid down some tracks for B.B. King, they expected to go home. But, daddy had other ideas. A song Larry wrote with Michael had caught Ray's attention. It sounded like something he had heard on the radio. Ray had decided to record the boy's song, and possibly, if it sounded right, he would make up some copies and distribute them.

That afternoon, with Michael playing drums and Larry playing base guitar, Ray laid down a song called "Jealous Girl In Town". Nineteen years later, "Jealous Girl In Town" would become a hit for New Edition, with Bobby Brown singing lead. That day, Larry sang his own composition and another tune he had written for the B-side entitled "Let Me Know What's On Your Mind". Ray made up four copies and sold them for a dollar apiece, and in one step, Larry was a composer and recording artist.

The intricate world of electronic recording opened up for Larry and his brother Michael. They would, through thousands of hours of practice and many years of dedication and recording studio time, become two of the more formidable record producers in R & B and rock and roll history. Their musical intelligence would span and retain music from the fifties, sixties, seventies, and eighties...and on, decades of musical changes, and ideas that would format their musical skills.

Already adept players, who could hear a song once, retain it, and play it. The Johnson boys would now be able to produce records. They could remember a Bo Diddley guitar riff from the fifties, or a Sly and the Family Stone horn-line from the sixties, or a Parliament Funkadelic bass line from the seventies, or a Madonna string-line from the eighties. Their musical passion, in retention of material, held no peer.

At twelve, Larry wrote a few songs that Donnie, Jordan, Jonathan, Danny and Joe would sing on their first album. That same year, he would become the Director of the Southwestern High School band; and be remembered as an exceptionally patient teacher. During these formative years, Larry and his brothers would perform at hundreds of church socials, private dances and talent shows throughout the Central Florida region. The brothers, at this time, were also exchanging instruments, becoming proficient on one instrument, and moving on to another; and they were developing their musical theory at a high rate of speed.

Larry would go from guitar to organ, to piano, to trombone, to violin, to trumpet, to harpsichord, to anything he could put his hands on, and lips to. In all, by the time he was fifteen, Larry could play—at a high degree of proficiency—a total of almost forty instruments!

Ray and Willie Mae had been successful in raising their family. The boys were not only professional musicians, but they were good kids. Elvin, Ray, Donald and Calvin had also turned into excellent building construction men and Larry and Michael were heavy into electronics. During these years, a few recording companies approached them. They had done some television and radio, and most of the promoters in the South had heard of the Johnson Brothers, knew them well, and had great respect for them. The Johnson Brothers were known for showing up for gigs on time with uniforms clean and shoes spit-shined to a glossy glow from which each brother could see his own face in his shoes. Oh, yeah! The Johnson Brothers could damn well play anything in sight and look good.

Ray's boys were "bad", but where were they going and what was next?

Chapter Eight
The Road To Riches

Larry, now fifteen, and playing for thirteen and a half years (five years as a professional) was ready to go further. The year was 1968, and rock and roll was happening. I mean, the greats were out there! Aretha Franklin, Sam and Dave, The Beatles, Jimi Hendrix, Sly, The Rolling Stones, Isaac Hayes, Carla and Rufus Thomas, James Brown, Joe Tex, and Otis Redding! Black radio was expanding and the youth of America were turned on to the Total Black Experience. Black was Beautiful! Black was in! Oh, yeah! The greats were out there; and a decision was made that it was time to get theirs. Ray and Willie Mae had given all they could to their boys...all the music and love they would provide, and now, the boys had surpassed them. Their schooling and direction in music had been superb. So, the decision was made. Larry would drop out of school at fifteen, and in the tenth grade and Michael, at fourteen, would follow.

The boys would hit the road working their way up North, using a variety of promoters and business people for their one-niters, using contacts and friends of their parents to gain lodging and bookings. Outfitted with a van, instruments and sound system, the boys hit it. They met and dealt with all kinds of people, from the shadiest to the most reliable. Pushing hard to get theirs, they left the South hoping to attract the attention of those big city record companies—a move that would ultimately destroy the group through its frustration. But, for Larry and Michael it would only increase their determination to go all the way to the top!

The Rise of New Kids on the Block...

Now on the road, these boys were no dummies. They were a highly efficient music machine ...able to crank out the music at a high volume of speed, out-think and out-maneuver any close calls along the way. Their home education, as well as the schooling they got, was intense. They were taught to be inquisitive, cautious and curious... to leave nothing to chance. To read and study was a way of life. Everything was assimilated. Larry and his brothers were sponges—soaking up every bit of information, retaining it, and locking it in for future use.

Ray, they loved. He was their source, their guiding strength. But Willie Mae was their inspiration. At the age of thirty, after all her sons were in school, Willie Mae went to college to become a teacher—first to Daytona Beach Community College, then to Bethune-Cookman College, where she earned a Bachelor of Science degree in 1968. She taught in Seminole County Public Schools for five years and received a certificate in specific learning disabilities from Stetson University. Yes! Willie Mae was strong... strong enough to let them go and to keep their spirits always at home, always coming back to her for advice, for love, for her dreams and for her belief in them.

There's an old saying that "love and respect begin at home"; and for the Johnson and Rayford families, that also meant education and knowledge. To be ignorant was to be sinful, as was not using the talents that God gave you. As Calvin Johnson said in 1974, "We study almost anything you can think of: psychology, music...you name it. Our home in Deland, Florida has more books than musical instruments, and we've got a lot of musical instruments".

The years 1969 and 1970 were possibly the greatest two years in modern day musical rock and roll and rhythm and blues history. Radio and its album-orientated FM format were replacing top forty, home of the 45rpm hits, rapidly. The album was supreme, and the bands making the music were the baddest in the world. The monster that was Led Zeppelin, with Jimmy Page and Robert Plant, was revving up a machine that would forever change how bands toured, calling it "Arena Rock". Man, there was Filmore East in New York City and Filmore West in San Francisco!

There was Janis Joplin (a white girl singing some heavy blues) from Texas, Jefferson Airplane, The Mamas and Papas, The Doors with Jim Morrison, Donovan, Simon and Garfunkel, and The Grateful Dead. Brian Jones was still alive and kicking with the Rolling Stones, and Mick Jagger and Keith were playing a symphony for the devil. The Beach Boys were making a comeback. Sly and the Family Stone were taking you higher. The Who would play a pin ball machine with Tommy; and The Beatles were the greatest! The best! The biggest! Only "to die for" were the Beatles, since "I Want to Hold Your Hand", in 1964, and Jimi Hendrix, the guitarist.

The screams from their millions of fans has never stopped. In concert, in life, on record...the Beatles were psychedelic, prisms of light. Oh! Paul, John, George and Ringo! That was another world, full of Peter Pan characters, of strawberry dreams and peppermint colors.

Down South, there was Stax, working with Ahmet Ertegun's Atlantic Records, cranking out those sweet soul sounds of Arthur Conway, Otis Redding, Wilson Pickett "Midnight Moving", Aretha Franklin getting respect, Percy Sledge singing "When A Man Loves A Woman", Issac Hayes Chained, Hot and Buttered and Souled, Sam and Dave "Holding On Forever" and The One, The Only, James Brown. And in Detroit, a guy named Berry Gordy, who had the Midas touch, had built the most awesome array of phenomenal talent, producers, songwriters, arrangers, musicians and artists that the world had ever seen...beginning with Smokey Robinson and the Miracles. Oh man! I'll just run the names for you. You know them and you know the songs. They're a part of American history...there, in the world, there on CD and DVD forever. They're Mary Wells, The Marvelettes, The Four Tops, The Supremes with Diana Ross. The Temptations, the magnificent Marvin Gaye, The

Isley Brothers, Junior Walker and the All Stars, Gladys Knight and The Pips, Martha and The Vandellas, Tammy Terrell, Stevie Wonder, and The Spinners. They're producers and songwriters, like: Holland/ Dozier and Holland, Norman Whitfield, J. J. Johnson, Harvey Fuqua, Clarence Paul, and Smokey Robinson.

Ask your mothers, hell ask your grandmothers, boys and girls. Go crawl up into daddy's or granddaddy's lap. They'll tell you! They know what time it was! This was the sixties; and the Johnson Brothers were riding right through it—hitting and quitting. They were one-nighting and weekending From Memphis to Washington, from North Carolina to Mississippi, up to Georgia, down to Florida, over to Tennessee. They were listening to the radio, learning Tyrone Davis tunes, setting up and breaking down, playing that "chittling circuit", which daddy had played twenty, thirty years before. And, Larry would see and hear the Beatles and remember the girls screaming and keep his ear to the ground, hearing about Berry's Motown operation where a young man named Dick Scott from Detroit was managing some of Berry's acts.

Larry was listening hard and playing fast. He was getting the hits down, mimicking voices, and playing note for note, right off the radio. They were psychedelic, in the land of wonder. And then the music died. The Beatles came to "Abbey Road" and talked about the long and winding road and Paul left and John left. George was disgusted and Ringo wanted to know where everybody had gone. Jim Morrison died in Paris; Jimi Hendrix kicked it in London; and Janis OD'd in New York City. It was 1970…and the sixties were over.

But, for Larry and the Johnson Brothers, something even more phenomenal had happened. Berry Gordy had moved out to Los Angeles in 1969. Now, Larry and the boys had sent a few demo tapes to Motown over the years, but they had received little response. Berry wasn't into southern bands. Besides, he already had Junior Walker and the All-Stars, and that was as gritty as he wanted to get. But, in 1969, Berry signed some brothers from Gary, Indiana. They had a lead singer named Michael who was ten years old, Marlon who was twelve years old, Jermaine who was thirteen years old and playing bass and guitar, Torian who was fourteen on lead guitar, Jackie who was sixteen…and they called themselves the Jackson Five. Man! They were "b-a-d"! and caught everyone unaware.

Larry, now seventeen, and Elvin, now twenty-four, felt old compared to them guys. Their backgrounds were almost the same, except that daddy Jackson had put them boys to work earlier; and had them riding around the country performing at the Apollo and everything, when Michael was just five years old. The success of the Jackson 5 would propel the Johnsons to New York City where they would bang on the big city company doors, demanding a deal and trying to get their shot. But, the Jacksons were younger, cuddlier, and had a smash hit entitled, "I Want You Back"; and, for the next three years, all you heard about was the Jackson 5.

The Johnsons kept on! It nearly broke their hearts, 'cause they figured that they were "badder" than anybody.' But, Larry saw and learned. He remembered how people took to the Jacksons, how they would pack a stadium and sell millions of records, and, their infectious melodies and songs, "ABC", "I'll Be There", "Who's Loving You"—all their hits—would forever linger in his head. And in 1982, he would write and produce "Candy Girl", a complete reworking of the Jackson 5's "ABC" with a young group from Roxbury, Massachusetts, similar in age and looks to the Jackson 5, called New Edition. "Candy Girl" would sell one million copies, and Maurice Starr would finally get his revenge for the pain that he and his brothers had suffered from 1970-1975, being called "the next best thing to the Jackson 5", The Johnsons; never making it that big, not even coming close—they kept working, but a little bit of their heart had been taken away.

The Rise of New Kids on the Block...

Chapter Nine
Paying Dues

During these years of one-niters, Larry and his brothers would meet a lot of influential people—radio deejays, record company executives, big-time promoters, small-time promoters, club owners and talent scouts. Always professional, they never lacked for television appearances and the local newspapers always seemed to find space for the handsome energetic brothers in the city entertainment section. Wherever they went, the Johnson Brothers were welcome. As one entertainment columnist said, "There is nothing too great I can say about the group. For a treat, check them out some time. They are exciting to the young, and keep the old excited".

Success was always just around the corner for the Johnson Brothers, and hard work was the key to unlocking that door. The Johnson Brothers worked hard loading and unloading equipment; keeping their show clothes clean and spiffy, playing hard all night for the people; practicing hard all day learning new hits to play at night. They traveled from city to city, town to town—the hard way. There were no planes, no big tour busses, no relaxing limos to lounge in, and no big record company support at all.

No, they had none of that. But they did have love. O, man! Did they have some love! The ladies, the sisters, the women, the girls, the lovelies, the sweet things, the sisters (young and old)! Lord, have mercy! The sisters came running. If they couldn't get to and jump all over Michael and the Jackson 5, well, here was the next best thing to it. And coming right to their back door, right up the street,

The Rise of New Kids on the Block...

appearing at The Doo Drop Inn Lounge, "The Johnson Brothers"! And, oh man, did they jump on them guys! Backstage, on stage, off the stage, around the stage. They were some bad musicians, you know, and the ladies like that. Hey, you know... "I'll do anything for you, baby, just sing me a little note in my ear". Or, "Ooh baby, whatever you want, just let me see you hit that guitar again." Or, "Oh baby, can I put my mouth on that horn, where you put yours?" Or, "Oh baby, are you gonna sing just to me tonight when you're on stage?" Hey man, the Johnsons didn't need no limos. They were personally chauffeured by the finest foxes in every city they hit. Individually, taken to the best soul food restaurants where they ate collard greens, mashed potatoes and gravy, pork chops and chicken, hominy grits and eggs—anytime they wanted—paid for by the sweet foxes; or the soul food restaurant owner personally said "No Charge", and a place to sleep after the gig, hey, listen "you come home with me baby, and you won't need no plane to take you to the next city. You'll be flying in that van of yours." Hey' and if the lounge or club owner couldn't, or wouldn't pay enough money, the fox would always chip in with some extra dollars.

No, the boys didn't worry about too much. There was always a Rayford or a Johnson, in most cities they played in, setting up their newspaper, radio and television interviews, seeing to their basic comforts and needs, checking their equipment out, replacing

Paying Dues

speakers or amps, fixing guitars, getting new strings or reeds, introducing them to local politicians and black businessmen.

The Johnson Brothers knew everything and everybody that was happening in every city they played. White guys, black guys, slick promoters, people with advice on how to make it, how to fix your hair, how to play, what to play, everybody knew somebody that could help out, help the Johnson Brothers get a step further. Radio deejays were gonna call record companies, managers wanted to manage, the producers wanted to produce them. Everybody saw the potential, everybody wanted a piece of the action, and the ladies were getting a little more than a piece of it, but nobody had the key to the magic door of success.....and the band played on.

The old song "The Boys Are Back in Town" performed by Thin Lizzy, could have been written about Larry and his brothers. People anticipated the return of the Johnsons. There was a certain charisma about them, and they were good. Larry, by now a skinny six-footer, had developed his own style of playing guitar. It was soulful and funky, with a lot of Bo Diddley, Chuck Berry and Sly Stone riffs with rapid chord changes. Larry could also switch to bass guitar, piano, drums, or horns—with perfect ease.

The main features of a Johnson Brothers engagement were their switching off and playing different instruments. They had a tightly choreographed dance routine for each song and repetitive shouts to get the crowd on their feet. Intricate and demanding musical performances, horns blowing hard in syncopated James Brown horn riffs, drums right on the one, the back beat heavy with the snare hits, the bass guitar making the floor shake, the keys sweet and melodic; and Larry on guitar and vocals looking, playing and singing, like every rhythm and blues guitar player and singer before him.

The Johnson Brothers lineup looked like this: Calvin singing alto, main instrument trumpet, plays ten instruments; Donald singing baritone, main instrument sax, plays twelve instruments; Elvin singing baritone, bass and soprano, main instrument piano, plays twenty instruments; Ray singing alto soprano, main instrument trumpet, plays twenty instruments; Michael singing alto and baritone, main instrument drums, plays forty instruments; and Larry writing, arranging and composing most of the group's material; singing alto, soprano, bass and baritone; main instrument guitar, plays forty instruments.

The show was a typical southern rhythm and blues revue, with lots of interaction on stage, clowning, mimicry, talking and choreographed dancing, every detail rehearsed over and over again. Their show's primary source was James Brown and the Famous Flames—musically and showmanship-wise, with a touch of everybody they saw, except the hated Jackson 5. An early article says it all: "The Johnson Brothers' sounds are concentrated in audience-orientated areas. Most renditions are easily recognized by the audience. Mike sings 'The Love I Lost' made popular by Harold Melvin and the Bluenotes and an uptemo 'Rock and Roll Baby'. Larry is featured wailin' 'Let's Get It On'—the current Marvin Gaye hit, followed by 'Here I Am Baby'—Al Green's chart-topper! And, you'd better believe that if you closed your eyes, you would have thought Marvin Gaye and Al Green were right there up on that stage singing to you." O yeah, no doubt about it, when Larry and the boys came to town, it rocked.

Down in Deland, Florida, Ray and Willie Mae were still dispersing advice and direction to the group. You could say they were the Johnson Brothers managers. In fact, you could say that the only managers the Johnson Brothers, Maurice Starr, and Michael Jonzun ever had was God, Ray and Willie Mae, and that's the truth, Ruth! Now the Johnson Brothers had been playing one-niters and weekenders out there on the road since 1968. It was now 1973, and some changes had come about.

Ray, Jr. had gotten married and was only occasionally playing with his brothers. Elvin, now twenty-six, and playing for twenty-two years, didn't see where it was going, and started using his building trade skills more and more. An effort was made to get the boys off the road, and give them a solid base from which they could launch the second phase of their career. Washington, DC was ruled out, because there were too many local bands and great musicians already on the scene. New York was too vast, and without a record company, where would they go? Down South was not the place to build a big name in the entertainment business and get paid.

Meetings were held and relatives' advice was sought out. The consensus was that the Johnson Brothers had been fairly successful in Central Florida, and on the road, and that a major push by the entire family would raise them over the top. An uncle, Arthur Rayford, a contract carpenter (who also played drums) had moved to Boston, Massachusetts, and was living in the black community of Roxbury.

The Rise of New Kids on the Block...

Part Three
The Boston Music Scene

The Rise of New Kids on the Block...

Chapter Ten
A New Base Is Built In Boston

In 1973, the city of Boston was enjoying a modern day renaissance. The city had a brilliant mayor who believed in helping all the neighborhoods, and that meant the black communities of Roxbury and Dorchester, as well. He established "Little City Halls" in Roxbury, Dorchester and Jamaica Plain; created "family life centers" and small health clinics directly tied to Boston City Hospital. Thus, the poor could receive pre-natal, dental, health, and emergency care right in their own neighborhoods. It was a brilliant idea that worked! Mayor Kevin White was also interested in bringing the black and white neighborhoods in Boston together.

The desegregation of Boston's Public Schools looked, at first, like the biggest mistake anybody could have ever made. Hatred, fear and racial prejudice ran rampant through the entire city. Mayor White was crushed. Boston, in one liberal move, one move of passionate change, had made Mayor White's "Boston" look on national television, like a dinosaur, an ancient relic of racial diversion, worse than any "good ole boy Southern town" in Alabama.

Mayor White would never forget the scorn and hatred heaped upon him. He would never rise again from that so-called folly. Nobody would ever ask him to run for governor, or talk about him as a possible vice-presidential candidate again. But, he would live and go on, and watch as one of his most intelligent and intricate ideas survived and flourished, weathering time, gaining more and more respect each year, until in 1988 he would listen, as Donnie told a crowd how he and three friends—Jordan, Jonathan, Danny—and hundreds of other kids like them, had been bussed to all black schools; and were grateful, not only for the education they had received, but for the friends they had made, the different cultures they had been exposed to, and the full enjoyment of respecting all the differences that make us human beings under one roof and one sun in God's eyes.

That day, Kevin White, listening and smiling, knew his plan had worked. Put some little kids—black and white—in kindergarten and the first grade together, and in twelve years, take a look at the results. Well, the results were showing up and looking good. The success of Mayor White would have historical implications of immense importance. These kids, called the New Kids on The Block, would forever change the thinking of an ethnic record industry. They would travel an entire world, telling people everywhere about a guy in Boston named Kevin White who desegregated Boston's schools, so that they could get to something different, and meet fate head-on. Standing beside them would be a guy that came to Boston as Larry Johnson, but was now the legendary Maurice Starr.

But, this was still 1973 and being black in Boston was a pretty good thing to be. Jobs were plentiful. The city government was open; and most important, good housing was cheap. The Johnsons and Rayfords had been coming to Boston for years, and knew the black community well. They were tradesmen and carpenters, into construction, buying up old houses and restoring them. Arthur Rayford knew a lot of people, and because he played drums, a lot of the people he knew were in the entertainment business.

Now, Boston had a substantial nightlife in the black community. There was the Sugar Shack in downtown Boston that featured some of the biggest names in black entertainment; Estelle's on Tremont Street, where Marvin Gaye had performed at the grand opening; Paul's Mall and the Jazz Workshop on Boylston Street; The great Northampton Street area clubs—Louie's Lounge, Basin Street, Shanty's, Doc's and Roscoe's (a club owned by a Southern black entrepreneur, Roscoe Gorham).

Arthur Rayford went to the managers and owners of the nightclubs and lounges, told them he had the greatest band they would ever hear, coming to Boston and asked if his boys could work in their clubs. When he called Ray and Willie Mae, Arthur told them the boys could get some solid work in the Boston and New England area, and he had a place for them to live—a house at 20 Linwood Square in Roxbury.

In 1973, Larry and his brothers loaded up everything lock, stock and barrel, leaving 233 East Howry Avenue, Deland, Florida for Roxbury, Massachusetts in Boston. It proved to be a dream come true. The Johnsons were a big fish in a little pond, because nobody (and I mean nobody—white band or black band) could out-play The Johnson Brothers in the entire New England area; and their name and fame increased rapidly.

But, Boston had not yet been discovered by the big, well-oiled recording industry machines. In fact, the biggest star to come out of the New England area during the great 60's/early 70's was a folk balladeer turned R & B revisionist, "Sweet Baby James Taylor" and his brother Livingston Taylor. The power-house group Aerosmith would not show up until 1976, the J. Geils Band was still local. the band Boston would roll, the summer of '76. Rick Osack and his group the Cars would mobilize in 1978; and the black community would feel pretty good when Roxburian Donna Summer made the charts in 1975, even though her success was a direct result of her having lived in Germany for two years. No, Boston had not been discovered yet. But, it was on the verge; and some major links were being locked into place.

Now Boston's black community was small, maybe sixty or sixty-five thousand people. The majority were living in Roxbury, Dorchester and Mattapan; and divided up into three factions: people whose families had arrived in Boston or New England during the early to late nineteenth century; families whose people had arrived from down South in the 1900's to 1920's; and people just arrived.

The first faction's family consisted of professors, lawyers, publishers and doctors. They were professional people, usually educated at Harvard, Columbia or Princeton. They were also the minority, living and socializing together; and they had great political influence. The second faction became city workers, government employees, or on state welfare. There were the majority, but very silent and had no power whatsoever. The third faction were skilled tradesmen and invigorating entrepreneurs, running candy stores and numbers; working in, and then owning gas stations and nightclubs; buying property and getting into real estate. These people were hard-working and determined men and women—skilled carpenters, masons and tradesmen—right out of the "New South". They had no fear of anyone, especially the white man. They were clannish and suspicious of the first faction; held no respect for the second faction; and knew that one day, they would be the majority and have the political power.

The community was small, but very divided. The Southern people decided they had to make their own way. The black bourgeois looked down on them, the native Roxburians were apathetic. It was an ideal place for an up and coming group to establish a base at….a strong black Southern community, who liked to party and had some money to spend.

Well, the Johnson Brothers settled in, doing college and club dates, all over New England and the East Coast. They appeared in places like: Old Orchard Beach in Maine, the Apollo Theater in New York City, they were booked by black and white club promoters from Connecticut to Vermont to Pennsylvania to New Hampshire. They were soon on the white circuit, and they were in big demand as studio session players, getting a name for having done some work for James and Livingston Taylor. The boys liked playing for the white promoters and doing work for the white producers and musicians; the money was good. But when they came back to Roxbury they'd play almost free for a guy, if his club needed the help. Larry and his brothers always had good hearts, and would definitely help you out if you were a friend of the Johnsons.

A New Base Is Built In Boston

But, that big time recording contract kept eluding them. One record company executive said years later, "Every time I wanted to sign them, they'd have something new to play for me. I could never pin them down into a market area. One day, they're country and western, the next time I'd talk to them, it would be rock 'n roll, then love ballads, then the funk, I couldn't sign them because the company didn't know how to sell them."

He was right. The Johnson Brothers were always changing. They were different individuals with different thoughts on how the music should be; and because of the extraordinary amount of music they had assimilated from the radio, over the years, it was hard for them to know what the real Johnson Brothers sound was. During this period, they spent a lot of time in various recording studios in and around the Boston area. Larry, who had been arranging and writing the group's songs since the beginning, was starting to hear Donnie and Elvin, and even Calvin's advice on how he should record or arrange something. It was becoming harder to play and record with his brothers. Maurice felt he was a genius, and that they should listen to only his ideas. Of course, the brothers had other thoughts, and so would perform at half their abilities.

The owners of Intermediate Recording Studio in Boston tried to manage them, giving them free studio time. They were going to release an album on the group, and had started lining up appearances for them on shows like "Soultrain", but that fell through.

In 1977, Ray and Elvin quit the band for good. They were replaced with Gordon Worthy, a cousin, and Wes, a guitar player and good friend. Larry changed his name to Maurice Starr and took to wearing scarves around his neck, wearing flamboyant clothes all the time, and giving himself a James Brown hairdo. The group would now be called the Johnson Brothers, featuring Maurice Starr. Maurice took to booking his own shows, with the help of an uncle named Obie Johnson, and they played for every politician, every benefit, every club—opening and closing shows (anywhere and everywhere)—writing songs; and when they were at home at Linwood Square, they would teach music to anyone that wanted to learn.

The Rise of New Kids on the Block...

Chapter Eleven
Maurice Starr Emerges to the Forefront

Maurice was making one last ditch effort to hold on to his group, trying anything that could get them a deal, he even wrote a couple of songs that he sent to the Massachusetts State Lottery (both were turned down). It was getting very difficult to keep the band together. Michael was fine. He'd follow Maurice anywhere, but Donnie and Calvin had other ideas. The gigs were slowing down. Everybody had made promises, but nobody had delivered. They had the name, but no fame, and no money.

Two things happened that decided the fate of the band. Dick Scott, a guy from Detroit who had managed some of Berry Gordy's acts, and (for a while there) Diana Ross herself, heard about a movie that was being made in Hollywood. He remembered Maurice and the Johnson Brothers, because of all the tapes they had sent to Motown Records and the other record companies all through the years. He had seen the Johnson's live, catching Maurice Starr's mimicry of Little Richard. There was a part in the movie for a singer to look like and imitate Little Richard, and Dick Scott recommended Maurice.

As Maurice Starr recalled, he first auditioned for the part for the producers, at Roxbury's Parker Street Lounge. He then went to compete in an auditioning session with some two hundred other hopefuls. Maurice won the part he says, because he was confident that he could deliver the type of performance that the producers wanted. In 1978 Maurice went to Hollywood for two weeks for the filming of "American Hot Wax".

While filming, Maurice sang Little Richard's "Tutti Fruitti", "Slippin and Slidin" and "Good Golly Miss Molly". He appears at the end of "American Hot Wax" on film, banging on a couple of trash cans; symbolizing that even though they could arrest Allen Freed, the music of rock and roll would never die. Maurice played the next generation coming up. He played those trash cans, all while the end credits were rolling, and you know he was something special, even then. Look at the role he was playing! The movie came out in 1979. It didn't do a lot, but Maurice felt good, and told everybody. And everybody in Roxbury went to see him.

Before the movie came out the band was getting even more edgy, with Donnie wanting to make a complete break. He had found some backers, and had been approached to do some pretty big projects. Maurice, wanting to still hold onto the band agreed to co-produce with Donnie a record, which a small company wanted to put out. The group would be Donnie Johnson and the Johnson Brothers. The record did come out, but it didn't receive the response that the brothers had hoped for.

Once again, they were crushed. Their egos told them they were as good as anybody out there, but they just couldn't get the right breaks, and the brothers began to blame each other. It looked like the band was about to break up, but Michael and Maurice came up with a good idea to start their own record company. They would press and distribute their own records. That way, they could record and play as the Johnson Brothers, and record and produce each other separately, utilizing their individual ideas. They would call the new record label Boston International Records; and Maurice Starr would be their first artist.

Chapter Twelve
The Legend Begins— The Birth of Boston International Records

In February 1979 an infectious sound hit the Boston airwaves. The radio announcer (Steve Crumbley) Program Director at W.I.L.D., Boston's only black radio station at the time, probably said something like this, "Boston, I've got something new for you. It's homegrown, and the man is standing right here with it. It's a new tune by Maurice Starr, and it's called 'About Time I Funk You'." Well, that did it! Finally Maurice was on the map and on the radio. He could be heard loud and clear…a song that he and baby brother Michael had written, produced, pressed up, and now, out for everybody to see and hear. This tune, a happy funk tune, with a baseline running wild with the Parliament Funkadelics, and a guitar riff being played at the speed of sound, and Baby brother Michael on the drums, hitting that snare so hard you might think it's going to break…. just like the old days. And, Maurice screaming "About Time I Funk You Baby, I Been Waiting So Long". Yeh, he'd been waiting a long time for this record, or any record, that could give him a name and fame. He took that record and personally hand-carried it to every radio station in Boston and Providence, making it the most-requested song on the air.

The Rise of New Kids on the Block...

That Spring "79", all the Boston "hip" stations played it.... WILD, WRBB, WUNR, WTBS, WERS.......all of them. Maurice was a celebrity. He had a hair weave put in his hair, was invited to sing "The National Anthem" at Providence Civic Center for a Muhammed Ali fight, his movie came out, and RCA Records gave him a recording contract and released "About Time I Funk You" backed on the B-Side with another funk tune he'd written called "Baby Come On (And Shake Your Rump)". Maurice Starr was on his way. The Johnson Brothers would really never regroup again, but they'd always be there when Maurice or Michael called. Sonny moved out of 20 Linwood Square, buying his own house. Elvin would come and go. But, Maurice, Michael and Calvin would stay together for a few more years.

Chapter Thirteen
Breaking Into The Big Time

Yeah boy! The summer of 1979 was unlike anything anybody had ever seen in Roxbury—the black community of Boston had come alive musically. On the other side of Boston—the white side—groups like the Cars, Boston, J. Geils Band, Aerosmith and others had already broken through the charts and had been making big money for years. But in Roxbury, groups like the Energetics (a group managed by a Southern nightclub owner named Roscoe Gorham) and the Ambitions fronted by Larry "Woo" Wedgeworth, a brilliant singer who would achieve success years later as a producer with Maurice Starr's cousin Gordon Worthy as Woo/Worthy Productions, and the now defunct Johnson Brothers were still struggling.

The Boston music scene was divided into two worlds—black and white. White was on top—and black was on the bottom. But, in 1979, a kid from Roxbury (Boston) who had gone to Los Angeles where he had hands-on training in the music business, came back home to Roxbury as a professional music industry person with knowledge of A & R, promotions, marketing, management, distribution and signing artists to major record labels. That 26-year-old kid, Tony Rose, woke up the local Roxbury Black musicians and showed them how to do it the Hollywood way. Then, Tony Rose met Maurice Starr and showed him that playing in nightclubs in and around Boston and banging on the record company doors with a cassette in his hand was not the way. Tony Rose got Maurice Starr and his single, "Bout Time, I Funk You, Baby", signed to RCA Records, a major record label. Prior to that, Tony had helped get a local group, the Energetics, signed to Atlantic Records, another major label. The Energetics would go on to make their first album, "Down to Earth," and the group later became Planet Patrol.

The Rise of New Kids on the Block...

Writers note: *(Maurice, Michael and myself would produce a 12" (twelve inch) single called "In the Streets" on a musician from Roxbury playing in Maurice's band. His name was Charles Alexander, but he would call himself Prince Charles and the City Beat Band. I would form a record company and release the 12" (twelve inch) record, using the same tactics as Maurice and Michael, and eventually sell the product to a major record company. This would be my beginning to establishing a recording and music publishing company, Solid Platinum Records and Productions, that would do business on an international level and make Prince Charles and the City Beat Band an international star during the early to late eighties).*

RCA released "Bout Time I Funk You" b/w "Baby Come On" as a 12" (twelve inch) single. Maurice put a band together with his brothers Michael on drums, Donnie on sax, and Calvin on trumpet, and friends Charles on keyboards, Stanley on guitar, and Steve on bass guitar.

Ray, Sr. and Willie Mae, unhappy about the break-up of the Johnson Brothers, but surprised and overjoyed about Maurice's signing with RCA, again, told the brothers that no one was more important than the other and that the greatest success lay in their helping and sticking by one another. To show their support, they sent up from Deland, Florida a brand new silver-grey van—big enough to hold equipment and band members, and at the Buffalo Civic Center, Ray Johnson, Sr. himself showed up to witness his son's first great triumph in the music world.

"Bout Time I Funk You" was a minor hit that everybody thought was gonna get even bigger everyday. RCA had a cracker-jack black promotional team headed by Ray Harris and Keith Jackson (they'd had enormous success with Shalamar, Midnight Star and Lakeside) that's what they told Maurice who was settling into doing a few concert dates and preparing for his first album. The truth was that the promotional department at RCA was not having success with "Bout Time I Funk You", Keith Jackson worked hard, because he knew Maurice, and he was from Boston.

But, Ray Harris was more involved with the Solar Record label, with its already established stars, so the big money push wasn't coming Maurice Starr's way, and somebody at RCA had told Maurice to stop doing his own publicity. So, Maurice sat at home, working on his first album while somebody else at RCA whispered in his ear that he should tone down on the funk. They told him that was why he wasn't getting mainstream radio play, that his songs and their titles were too risqué, and Maurice listened. He stopped doing his own promotion and concentrated on writing lyrics and music that didn't have that harder edge.

Maurice listened, and Michael (now calling himself Michael Jonzun) and Roscoe Gorham, supplying the recording budget, set to work at Intermediate Recording Studio on Newbury Street in Boston recording an album. Well, everybody from Roxbury participated—playing, singing, criticizing, sitting, watching, and listening. It was big! Although Maurice was not sure if RCA was going to pick up the album, Roscoe supplied the money, and the work progressed. Certain people felt that the album should be full of the funk and nothing but the funk, but RCA still felt that Maurice should water it down and become more mainline, even though Maurice himself was the funkiest cat outside of George Clinton alive.

Maurice was living at 20 Linwood Square (a big old house with "God knows who" running around it night and day) and wearing those "out of this world" costumes and capes with that hairweave in his head. He had the most infectious laugh you ever heard. In fact, the only time Maurice wasn't laughing or talking to some girl was when he was in the studio, and Calvin, Donnie, or Elvin would say something to criticize the music that he and Michael would be laying down. 'Cause, you know Maurice could play an instrument, sing, play around with the girls and laugh, all at the same time.

So, Maurice listened to the suits at RCA; and wrote and produced with Michael, some watered-down funk and some pretty good ballads. The album would be called Maurice Starr "Flaming Starr" showing Maurice on the cover in a silver jumpsuit with a red cape, silver lining and his trademark silk handkerchief around his neck. His hair was weaved perfectly, and a great smile of anticipation is on his face as bursts out of a flaming star. The tunes were "Moving On Up", "I Wanna Dance With You", "Come See Me Sometime", Start All Over", "Dance To The Funky Groove", "When I Say I Love You", You're The One (What's Your Name)", and "In My Life". Left off the album was "About Time I Funk You", "Baby Come On", and a tune (so funky that it made hard-core funksteers go "O man!") called "Fever In The Funkhouse". The opening lyrics went like this, "There's a fever in the funkhouse, there's a whole lot of funken going on"; and at the end, Maurice is screaming "Gonna funk you up, just give me the funk, gonna funk you up!". Yes, they left this off the album. Listening to the "suits", the album would bomb big. Maurice lost his credibility, and he lost the funk audience that he had built up in Boston, Buffalo, Cleveland and Baltimore. All this hard work went down the drain in one fast motion.

Breaking Into The Big Time

Prince Charles and the City Beat Band (the group Maurice had helped launch) took over his funk mantle, going from the streets of Roxbury to Madison Square Garden to London's Wembley Stadium, touring around the world, using the same funk riffs Maurice had started out with. Maurice watched this happen, and although he tried, he never regained his funk audience again.

During this same period, Michael Jonzun cut a record for Brunswick Records, but, nobody bought that one either. The brothers had almost made it, but they had listened to the wrong people—a mistake they would try very hard not to repeat ever again.

Now, Maurice Starr had the name, but no fame, no fans and no money. Certain people he had counted on to help him push his new album hadn't come through, and he swore he'd get them. One day they'd beg to do business with him—he swore it. But, Michael and Maurice had finally, firmly established themselves as competent producers and songwriters who could deliver excellent music fast.

Near the end of 1980, real life for Maurice Starr and his brother Michael looked like this: It was that simple—back to square one—

The Rise of New Kids on the Block...

back to Doc's. Doc's was a bar on the corner of Harrison Avenue and Northampton Place. It was a "joint" with tables and chairs, "down-home" people, and bad liquor. The Johnson Brothers had played there back in the old days, and Maurice Starr was their hero. It didn't matter what happened out there in the world. In Doc's, it was always night, and you were always down South. The people cheered and cheered. They cheered some more for that boy, brought him back to life, and gave him an infusion of their soul; and Maurice gave them the hits—from the late sixties and seventies, that is. He gave them Tyrone Davis ("If I Could Turn Back the Hands of Time"), Luther Ingram ("If Loving You is Wrong, I Don't Wanna Be Right"), Joe Tex ("Skinny Legs and All"), Otis Redding ("Sitting On The Dock Of The Bay") Teddy Pendergrass, Al Green, Johnnie Taylor ("Disco Lady")….all the hits …sounding just like them "Cats" were there. The crowd was hollering and screaming and Maurice was sitting up there on the stage with an organ in one hand and an old Moog synthesizer in the other. His eyes were half-closed and his hand touched the keys just right, just like mama had taught him with his left hand playing the bass and his right hand playing the chords and melody.

Maurice was singing for his life with the crowd yelling, all that smoke in the air….and Maurice is singing. There were no roadies, no big record company executives hearing the "real thing:", no radio people, no nobodies, no somebodies. Damn! He was riding that train alone again, and baby brother Michael was hitting that backbeat right on the one. Man! Them "cats" sounded like a ten-piece band up there at Doc's, and the people cheered and stomped their feet forever. I know! I was one of the lucky one's, I was there. They'd load up the van at 4:00 in the morning, then go back to 20 Linwood Street… with some girls… Michael said they were just rehearsing…Doc's was their rehearsal spot.

Hey! Things were happening in Roxbury—musical things. Dudes and dudettes were seriously going after recording contracts. There were, Lewis West and his Electric Power Band, Larry Wedgeworth, Arthur

Breaking Into The Big Time

Baker, Prince Charles and the City Beat Band, The Hypnotics, Dr. Funkenchain, Sargent Funk and Eric Nuri "the jazzman". Maurice had opened up a can of worms, and everybody was coming out to play—all the freaks—funny "cats" with weird hairdos and strange names, competing to see who was the "baddest" group in Boston.

Mary Alford (early NKOTB manager) at a Club 51 party with Prince Charles, Larry "Woo" Wedgeworth, unknown party-guest and Margo Thunder & Entrigue (right back) – 1981

Included were Margo Thunder, Wanda and Leslie, who were managed and kept in style by a white girl from North Dorchester named Mary Alford. Mary came on the scene in Roxbury; outfitted that wild Margo and the girls; put them on the stage in the heart of Roxbury (Dudley Street Station area) at a place called Roscoe's. Margo and the girls tore that stage up.

In the audience at Roscoe's, Corteez and the Rise Club would be all the "cats" coming to check out the latest and the greatest. You would hear: "Ladies and gentlemen, the Electric Power Band"; "Ladies and gentlemen, Prince Charles and the City Beat Band", "Ladies and gentlemen, Maurice Starr", "Ladies and gentlemen, Margo Thunder and Entrigue". Every Thursday, Friday and Saturday—up and down Blue Hill Avenue, down Washington Street, up Warren Street, up Massachusetts Avenue to the Rise Club in Cambridge—you heard "Ladies and gentlemen, Michael Jonzun!"

The scene in Roxbury was hot! Them "cats' were playing, the stakes were too high. Everybody had a killer instinct. Me and a "fly-girl" named Yvonne Willis soon to be Yvonne Rose gave parties 'til the sun" came up or the police came. All the baddest musicians, producers, agents and freaks came to those parties at "Club 51".

The Johnsons had picked Roxbury to live in because it was backward and divided. They felt that nobody in Boston came close to their musical abilities, and Roxbury was their own special playground. The people in the community were there to serve one cause—the Johnson Brothers cause—and Maurice went one step further, he wanted complete adoration, and all the money. It would take him another eight years, but he'd get it, and he'd get it all!

But, by the end of 1980, he must have thought there was a roller-coaster riding over his face. There were so many acts racing to be the first to make it, and make it big. So, he retreated to 20 Linwood Square, recorded some tapes, pulled out some old songs, listened to some new music, brooded a little, called Michael upstairs, and made some calls.

Sylvia Robinson performed and recorded as the Sylvia part of "Mickey and Silvia", hit makers in the fifties. Her singing voice had a sweet purring cat sound, like she could rip the shirt right off your back. In the sixties, Sylvia had married a shrewd black businessman named Joe Robinson. Together, they formed All-Platinum Records, hitting it big in the sixties and early seventies with a group called the

Moments. By 1979, they had changed the name of the record company to Sugar Hill Records, and had a two-million selling rap single called "Sugar Hill Rap", (originally written, produced and released as "Good Times" by Nile Rodgers and Bernard Edwards) for their group called the Sugar Hill Gang. It was the biggest selling rap record in history, up until Tone Loc's "Wild Thing".

So, when Maurice called, and finally got Sylvia on the line, he had also been listening to some even newer and hipper music than the funk. It was called "rap"; and in 1980, 1981, its heroes were Curtis Blow, Grandmaster Flash and the Furious Five, and the Sugar Hill Gang. Maurice looking for something new had discovered it on the radio and decided he could do it better—make it more musical. So he wrote a rap. The two biggest rap acts—Grandmaster Flash and the Furious Five and the Sugarhill Gang—were both on Sugar Hill Records. So, Maurice, getting real smart now, trying to come up with ways to separate himself from the come-uppers, used his extremely versatile musical intelligence and contrived a song to fit an act perfectly. It was a rap song that would pit the Sugar Hill Gang against the Furious Five. The rap song written by Maurice and Michael would set the standard for years, whereby any rap act would scream and shout about how bad they were, better than the other "Sucker MC's". The rap song was called "Showdown". It came out on the second Sugar Hill Gang album called "8th Wonder" in 1981. The opening lyrics said:

> Do you wanna have a party? Do you wanna have a ball?
> Do you wanna make the scene? Then scream".........

It was a complete party record, recorded at Sweet Mountain Studios in Englewood, with Sylvia giving herself writing credits, along with brother Michael. This recording absolutely established Maurice and Michael in the recording industry, as songwriters capable of writing for others besides themselves, and it gave them back their rightful place at the head of the table in the Roxbury music scene as the first to have written for a national act like Sugarhill Gang. However, the album would not be a hit, in fact it would be the demise of the Sugar Hill Gang. But, more important than that, Maurice and Michael got paid. Sylvia paid them boys $14,000 for that song. They got paid, and big time money! More than anybody else on the Roxbury scene had been paid! Yes, they got $14,000! Even though Sylvia embarrassed them, told them to get out of her studio when they tried to take over the production, and sent them home. Hey, she paid them $14,000. Man, it was big news in Roxbury! And all the music people said, "O man, Maurice!"

And baby brother Michael would use every dime to buy some eight-track recording equipment—a board, tape deck, effect units and compressors. Hey! Mike went to the music store for real! And Elvin took the third floor apart and brought in some wood, some noise reduction material, hammers and drills, and them boys—the Johnson Brothers—built themselves and put in an eight-track full-equipped recording studio, control room and studio room right in their house at 20 Linwood Square.

The studio was stocked with keyboards, guitars, synthesizers, horns and mikes. Michael's trusty drums in the studio room where Michael could lay down the beat all day and all night. Maurice plugged in, going direct, laying down that heavy bass sound (you know it by now) and some guitar on tape. Hey, it's always five o'clock in the morning; and some girls are still in there singing at Boston International Recording Studio....and them boys—Maurice and Michael—never did stop recording, thanks to Sylvia Robinson.

Ray and Willie Mae had always supported the boys, financially as well as spiritually. Their uncles Arthur and Elvin Rayford had befriended the brothers, even going so far as to make sure that the boys always had a place to stay at 20 Linwood Square, no matter what. The brothers were definitely worth it, and deeply grateful. Their spiritual belief in God never wavered, and they remained positive, even though they had no money left after Michael bought all that equipment and the studio was built. But it didn't matter. They had Family, and, all the girls that could sing, thought they could sing, wanted to sing, weren't sure if they could sing, might want to sing, or hey, if Maurice told them they could sing (and even if they had to do a little bit more than sing), well, at least the house stayed clean (well I won't say clean, but at least it stayed there), and Kentucky Fried Chicken was "only up the way if you give me a ride". So things were fine, and Maurice sat up there and watched and waited.

And Michael practically lived in that 8-track studio on the third floor…I mean, he lived in it. The other brothers started coming over, and before you knew it, the Johnson Brothers were playing again— only, they were playing in Michael and Maurice's studio. So now, they got the studio and were making music. So, the boys decided that it was time to put out another record on Boston International Records. And Maurice wrote, arranged and produced what, probably, is the funniest record ever made in recorded music history.

The record starts off with Maurice saying "Come on baby, let's go." The girl says "um". Maurice says "Get your pocketbook, come on girl". (Footsteps, doors slamming. It's at night, and Maurice is in a hurry) The girl says, "Are you sure you love me?" Maurice says, "Yeah, come on, let's go". (Another door slams. You can hear the girl's jewelry) The girl says, "Um", as she is being hustled up the stairs. (You know it's at 20 Linwood Square) Maurice says, "Come on". (The girl is frightened, but she's with Maurice, so it's alright). Maurice says "You got the money?" The girls says "Ya!" Pretty soon, a dog starts barking; springs start moving on the bed. The girl says "Oh!" (Lots of action is going on—bed creaking, dogs barking, Maurice and the girl making noises.

All of a sudden, you hear a siren.) Maurice says, "Get down, get down". The girl says, "What's that? What's that?" (The siren's getting loser) Maurice says, "It's the police. Don't worry about that. Keep your head down." The girl says, "Oh!" (like something's in her mouth) Maurice says, "Put your head down woman, don't look up!" (Lot's of noise, somebody breaking down the door. Maurice and the girl running out of the house, going through the bushes. Dogs barking, Elvin making noises) Michael says, "Thought you were going to get away, didn't you?" Maurice says, "Officer, I didn't know she was Underage, I thought she was 21."

This record is not only ingenious, for its usage of sound effects, and the fact that Maurice plays himself and the girl, but it's absolutely hysterical. It was pressed up and released, and paid for by good old Roscoe Gorham. It came out as the "Johnson's featuring Maurice Starr" and the title of the tune is "Jailbait, Part II" on Boston International Records (BIRI2009-b). It's seven minutes of the funkiest, funniest music you've ever heard in your life—a take off of the Ohio Players "Funky Worm" and Zapp's "More Bounce To The Ounce".

This record is most likely out of issue, but if anybody wants to send me their names and addresses, I'll make up a CD for you. (Please send five dollars).

Well, the record came out, and Maurice and the brothers didn't push it too hard. They were probably the only ones not laughing in Roxbury. Oh, the most important factor out of that experience was Michael Jonzun's usage of the vocorder, an effects unit made popular by Roger Trotman of the group Zapp. This effect unit would, a few year later, make Michael an authentic urban superstar and a pretty rich guy.

Near the end of 1981, everybody was having a great time in Roxbury. There were parties, concerts and shows, and independent records were being put out. It was a great time to be black, and to live in Roxbury. There was something in the air—something magical, like a rabbit was going to be pulled out of a hat. And now, boys and girls, let me tell you a story of a great significance of enormous proportions…a story filled with dreams, hopes, magic and (more important than anything) fate. And now, let me tell you what happened.

Chapter Fourteen
The Story Unfolds

The stage was set. The characters were coming out to play, and school was almost over in Roxbury. Those that had had some success on a local level were stepping out, going down to New York City, talking big, making big noises at the big record companies; or just spreading their wings a little, checking it all out—having paid dues in Roxbury—learning radio promotion, in-store record promotion and how to flash and shine a lot. One of these people was Arthur Baker, a white Jewish streetwise guy in the tradition of Morris Levy of Roulette Records, the Chess Brothers of Chicago and Tom Silverman of Tommy Boy Records. Arthur Baker, hanging around in Roxbury, learning (some say) everything he knew about production from Maurice Starr, moved to New York City with his wife Tina, to break out, do something on his own, without the shadow of Maurice and some other "cats" from Roxbury.

Meanwhile, back in Roxbury, Maurice—seeking to keep his name in the local limelight, and to keep some change in this pocket—took a look at a local production called the "Celebrity Award Show", recalled his beginnings doing talent shows in Deland, Florida, got with Roscoe Gorham to begin producing talent shows at Roscoe's Lounge on Warren Street (right around the corner from the Orchard Park Projects) in Roxbury. Maurice came up with the suitably flashy "The Hollywood Talent Night", a take-off from the "Celebrity Award Shows" which boasted the slogan "The Night Hollywood Comes To You". He held his talent shows in September and October, on Sundays at 2:00 in the afternoon, at Roscoe's.

The Rise of New Kids on the Block...

Singers, dancers, girl groups, little kids, big kids and adults came to Roscoe's to sit, drink, socialize and watch the local entertainment. People were getting used to seeing things happen in Roxbury.

Prince Charles, Maurice Starr and Tony Rose – 1980

Maurice Starr presents "The Hollywood Talent Night" preliminary auditions were held every Sunday at Roscoe's Lounge. First, second and third place winners would perform Sunday, November 21st 1981 at the Strand Theater in Dorchester. The first place winner would receive a recording contract with Boston International Recording Studio.

What began as a promotional gimmick for Boston International Records (to hopefully raise some money by getting people to record in the studio, so they could put out some records) turned into the magic key that would open the door to success. Because you see, Maurice met four kids from the Orchard Park Projects (a not particularly gracious place to live—in fact a down-right unhealthy environment) a real ghetto project from which few, if any, brothers and sisters really ever escaped from.

Well, these kids were in the hallways doing dance steps, singing along to records, being kids –but sharp, you could see it in their eyes. They listened to WILD Radio (1090 AM) all day, and they knew Roxbury was becoming hip. A lot of people were getting over. A lot of people who looked like them, came from where they came from, and lived right in the neighborhood...hey, practically next door to them.

So, on Sunday—dressed to kill, clean as they could be, and project-hallway rehearsed—Little Richard (Ricky) Bell, Michael Bivens, Ralph Tresvant and twelve year old Bobby Brown (along with assorted relatives and friends) made their way across the street to Roscoe's Lounge, got up on the stage, lip-sync'd to a record, came in first-place, were invited to the finals in November at the Strand Theatre, and met Maurice Starr.

Maurice called up his friends and contemporaries in Roxbury's music industry, to judge his talent show at the Strand. I was one of them. Here's what I saw: "Michael and the other Johnson Brothers, setting up the sound system...late, but getting it together... Maurice at the front (the box office), ready to M.C., get it over with, make some money, get a winner, go home...show started. Maurice on stage MC'ing calling the acts, naming them....girls, guys, dancers, singers, group, and then..."Ladies and Gentlemen! From the Orchard Park Projects in Roxbury, The New Edition!"

This was their second time on stage; and the boys were going to make the most of it. Everybody from the projects was there. I noticed it, and I'm sure Maurice did...especially at the box office when he counted the receipts. Well, the newly-named New Edition hit it! They were dancing, lip sync'ing...cute little kids with the audience making a lot of noise. They had something, got me excited, I voted for them! Show's over! They lost...came in second. Everybody's saying Maurice rigged it! I meet with the boys, say

"Hey, I'll come see you, talk to you." They appreciate it, leave with Travis Gorham and Brook Payne—their young managers.

I've got my group, Prince Charles and the City Beat Band, signed in New York to a production deal for my company Solid Platinum Records and Productions with John Luongo and Steven Machat on their label Pavilion, distributed by CBS Records. I'm busy. The album "Gang War" is out, we're starting to hit it big, and I've got a new record called "Beat the Bush" by Slyck coming out also on Solid Platinum Records—based in Roxbury, but I mention the group New Edition to Steve Machat, hoping he wants to do something with them, so that I can get a piece of the action and produce them.

Maurice told a magazine later that the guy who came in first didn't want to sign a contract with him. What happened is that Maurice went home, pulled out some old tapes, thought about Motown—and particularly his old nemesis the Jackson Five—and said, "Damn, Michael, what if we put together a Jackson Five. Let's take those kids put one more guy with them, use some of our old songs, and make them sound like the Jackson 5. Hey, man! We can do it right here! Let's write some new songs, bring them over, and teach them how to really sing."

Well, nobody else in Roxbury could have done it. They had the studio, they could record all they wanted to, and they had the background and the experience. They understood kids, because essentially Maurice and Michael were still operating at a childlike mentality. They had retained the memories of themselves as child performers, and related to music by seeing images in sound and lyrics much as a ghetto child would, and they knew the music of that Jackson 5 era backwards and forwards, having been forced to play it while traveling as the Johnson Brothers for years.

So the winner was dumped; and the second-place New Edition were brought into Boston International Records to begin music education school, as taught by Maurice Starr and Michael Jonzun…the same school that Donnie Wahlberg, Jordan Knight, Jonathan Knight, Danny Wood and Joey McIntyre would attend three years later. This school gave you a crash course in harmony, vocal phrasing, five part harmony, music theory, solo singing, chordal training, how-to hit a note right, group dancing and choreography, how to handle an instrument and play a few chords. They learned from the combined music business experiences (good and bad) of the Johnson Brothers, Michael Jonzun and Maurice Starr; how to get Kentucky Friend Chicken and UGI's Steak and Cheese, what a freak is, and, in short, how to make great music in the shortest amount of time, with two of the funniest, funkiest, genius musicians that ever lived.

So, Maurice wrote "Candy Girl" a great copy of the Jackson Five hit: "ABC", and in quick succession, he recorded several other top tunes. Some of them, which he wrote at age 10, 11 and 12, would eventually be called "Black Bubble Gum Music"; and the New Edition would become the first black pre-teen "Bubble Gum Group" to hit the national charts since the Jackson Five.

The Rise of New Kids on the Block...

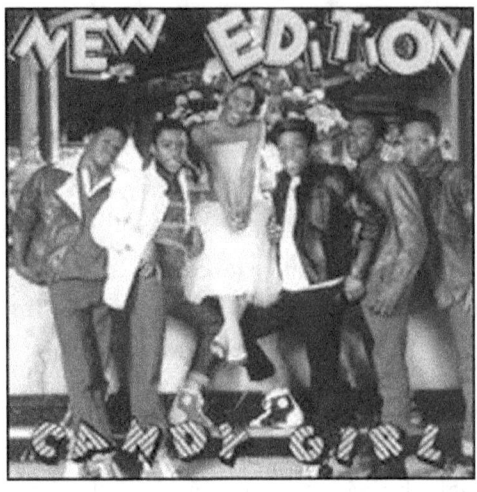

Maurice called every record company in New York; called all his friends, called everybody, playing their songs for them over the phone. Ralph, Ricky, Michael, Bobby, and soon Ronald Devoe, learning each note, singing, and what notes they couldn't hit—well, Maurice could and did sing that part. So.... the New Edition and the New Kids on the Block always had a sixth member, named Maurice Starr.

Meanwhile, in New York City, Arthur Baker was helping a few of his friends from Roxbury, get some record deals and sell a few records (for a few points on the record). He was involved, and had made a lot of connections, especially in the Jewish-owned companies. Maurice and Arthur did a couple of records for Posse-Spring Records. One was a pretty good funk record that didn't sell, called "We Come To Jam". Maurice sang lead, but the group was the Electric Power band, now called Blaze, on that record. They weren't successful with those projects, but Maurice appreciated the thought, and then it happened! Tom Silverman, who owned a music publication called "Dance Music Report", formed Tommy Boy Records, and released a twelve inch (12") record on a rapper, called "Jazzy J". The record did some business, selling in New York, and Tom learned. Arthur found a studio in New York called Intergalactic Recording Studios run by some friends of his (Rob and Chris) who gave him some real cheap studio time to do some projects, hoping he would bring in some more friends.

Maurice, in the meantime, finished up an album's worth of material on the New Edition, and baby brother Michael started a song that would take, as its theme, one of the most popular video games of the day. Arthur Baker's favorite record was "Trans Europe Express" by Kraftwork (a German group). It was very mechanical, very electronic, just right for the electric drum machines that were becoming Arthur Baker's instrument of choice. Times were changing. Real drummers were out, electronics were in, synthesizers with multi pre-set programmers were the rage, and in one flash—one moment of brilliance—Arthur put Trans Europe Express on the drum machine; called John Robie, a keyboard synthesizer wiz, and went deep into the Bronx and came out with a hard-looking' dude who called himself Africa Bambatta and who had a crew called the Soul-Sonic Force. Arthur got together with Tom, and wrote up some contracts. With Tom Silverman paying the bills at Intergalactic Recording Studio, Arthur Baker was in there night and day, E-Q'ing and mixing that bad boy to death. Tom says, "He's got something unique coming out", tells everybody and borrows and scrapes money up from relatives and friends…everybody… so that he can press up, distribute and promote this new sound. (This is the second record that he's going to put out on his Tommy Boy Records).

Well, boys and girls, ladies and gentlemen, that record was called "Planet Rock" by Africa Bambatta and the Soul Sonic Force; and it changed the whole configuration of music that summer. Two white Jewish fellows had combined electronics, Euro-tech, funk and rap; creating a whole new sound. It made them boys rich! And, in Boston, Michael Jonzun heard it, and said "Arthur Baker!" and he and Maurice shook their heads. Michael said "I can do that!" He called up Roscoe Gorham. Roscoe said yeah", he'd do another record with him. Michael called up Steve Thorpe (a friend) and Gordon Worthy (his cousin) and told them he was starting a group—no acoustics, all electronic. Released on Boston International Records in Roxbury on WILD-Radio, phones lit up, the request line was open; and Michael had a local hit.

Tom Silverman, riding hard that summer with "Planet Rock" heard about it through Arthur Baker. Arthur said that it sounded like "Planet Rock". Michael Jonzun, Roscoe Gorham and Marc Weiner (Roscoe's lawyer) went down to New York, talked to Tom, and signed a contract with Tommy Boy Records for Worldwide Distribution. Tom released it that summer (1982). The record was a twelve inch (12") record like "Planet Rock". The group was called the Jonzun Crew and the record was called "Pac Jam", and electronic take off on the PacMan video. It was the third biggest record of the year.

Meanwhile, Arthur Baker's making hand-over-fist money as the writer, producer, publisher and co-owner of "Planet Rock" and decides to form a record company with a couple of friends—a black guy named Paul McCraven (who had been living with him and Tina) and his rich white girlfriend Kathy Jacobson. They called the company "Streetwise Records", released a cut on a group called "Rockers Revenge" that does okay, and waited.

Meanwhile, back in Boston, Maurice Starr is having a fit. Baby brother Michael's got a hit. Arthur Baker's got a hit and started a record company, and he can't give away this five kid singing group! Maurice called and played that tape for everybody, but nobody wanted to touch it. Maurice was told that his idea was wrong; kid groups were out! That was yesterday stuff—five black kids singing! Nobody wanted to see that! This was the time of bands, rock and roll, funk and rap! Who would buy records by five little black kids?

Well, Arthur Baker, loving Maurice's sound, thought he'd take a chance. Maurice made a few changes, brought it to New York and did the deal with Streetwise Records. Arthur Baker wanted co-production and some publishing. Maurice said "Fine. Can you put it out?" And that summer, "Candy Girl", Candy Girl you're my world, sugar sweet, can't be beat", with Bobby Brown doing rap, came out. That summer, Michael Jonzun with Tom Silverman, Arthur Baker with Tom Silverman, Maurice Starr with Arthur Baker, and Tony Rose with Neil Cooper and Charles Alexander, hit it big!

All Spring, Summer, and Fall—all you heard on the radio was "Candy Girl", Planet Rock", "PacJam", "Bush Beat" by Slyck and "Jungle Stomp"—the number 1, 2, 3, 4 and 5 most requested records in radio-land. They were the most played and bought records from Harlem to Watts, from the Bronx to Miami, from Roxbury to Chicago. The boys from Roxbury were in Billboard Magazine, Record World and Cash Box on the charts. "Candy Girl" was number 1 on the black charts. The albums followed: "Candy Girl" by New Edition, "Planet Rock" by Africa Bambatta and the Soulsonic Force, "Lost in Space" by the Jonzun Crew and "Stone Killers" by Prince Charles and the City Beat Band. It was the big time, done on an independent level. The boys from Roxburywere selling millions of records; and the door was wide open.

But, there was a clink in Maurice Starr's armor. For one thing, Ricky Bell, Ralph Tresvant, Ronnie Devoe and Michael Bivens didn't come from the front-line Roxbury families, nor did they come from the recent Southern arrivals. They came from a part of Roxbury—ghettoized, poor, welfare- ridden, crime-depressed, drug-infested and no loyalty people who only had one scheme—to get rich quick. Whether it was playing numbers, selling drugs, conning somebody, hey! Hurting somebody bad! It didn't matter! What mattered was Numero Uno (Number 1). This was the other side of Roxbury…the bad side.

The Rise of New Kids on the Block...

Chapter Fifteen
Fall From Grace

Loyalty was scarce; and there was little, if any, team play—especially among the majority. Of course, Maurice didn't know this. He had been sheltered in a music world, and growing up in a fiercely loyal family, he didn't have the faintest idea of who and what those people were. All he did was give those little kids everything he had, wrote them great songs, gave them all of his musical abilities, gave them a sound, shared with them everything—his studio, his instruments—gave them hope, and they believed in Maurice. Those five kids—The New Edition—loved Maurice.

But, Maurice also had to deal with the parents or step-parents or mothers or boy friends, uncles, cousins, sisters, brothers, man, everybody was related to those boys. Everybody was coming out of the bricks with their hands out, looking for a free ride, looking for some money.

Now, Maurice had signed a personal management agreement with the boys, which their parents also had to sign; and Streetwise Records, at first, just signed Ralph Tresvant, who was the lead-singer and had the best voice. As far as Arthur Baker was concerned, the New Edition was really Maurice Starr, and in 1982 and 1983, it was. The boys really couldn't sing yet, so Maurice would fill in and sing their parts, and show them how to dance, too.

Arthur finally signed the other boys to a contract, separate from Ralph's. Maurice got the boys their first gigs at the Lee School in

Dorchester, South End Boy's Club, The Orchard Park Community Center, The Bromley Heath Housing Project and Northeastern University. Arthur was busy breaking the record in New York, and on February 5, 1983, the New Edition busted into the Copacabana Night Club in New York City. The New Edition broke nationwide and Maurice Starr began traveling with them.

Well, everybody in Roxbury just knew they were all gonna be rich, and right now! They didn't know that Maurice, as the manager, producer, songwriter and publisher was gonna make the real money (as well he should), since without his having put this together, nobody would have been talking about making money anyway. And, they didn't know that Streetwise Records, a small record company, although making money, was putting a lot of it back into the company to press and distribute more records. And, they didn't know that the boys had real low royalties. In fact, because Ralph had been signed alone to Streetwise Records, his royalty was equal to the other four combined.

In 1983, Maurice made (in record royalties) $60,859; and the New Edition made collectively) $41,975; and people in Roxbury were saying, "Hey Maurice, how come we ain't getting rich? Hey Maurice, the record's selling big!" The boys were traveling all over, lip syncing; people were calling "Hey, look man, they're in all the magazines, on television, doing interviews." People are calling, "Hey Maurice, how come we ain't getting rich?" In the meantime, Cynthia Horner, the editor from *"Right On!" Magazine,* practically discovers and adopts them, featuring them every month in America's number 1 black teen magazine, and Gheryl Busby, an up and coming record executive at the west coast based MCA Records starts listening to his daughter, telling him about this kid group back East that she's reading about in *Right On! Magazine.*

Back home in Roxbury, Maurice's life is being threatened. He can't believe it…. all he's done is try to help some kids. Hey, he wants to be rich and famous, too! And, hey we can do it if we all stick together. But, the people in Roxbury thought he was pulling a fast one on the boys; and what had they done? Nothing! But, they were definitely looking for some free money. Maurice later learned that it was called "the welfare check mentality". They were threatening Maurice Starr's life. Hey, the New Edition were all on TV, in the newspapers, all over the radio, with records running out at the record stores, doing concerts, and they were still living in the projects!

Well, Gheryl Busby investigated and went to his bosses at MCA Records, Los Angeles, California. They gave him a budget; and as Roxbury folklore goes "One night in 1983, people went to bed, woke up, and the Bell, Brown, Tresvante, Bivens and Devoe families had ceased to exist in the Orchard Park projects. The apartments were empty. The furniture was gone, and so were The New Edition; there wasn't even dust on the project floor. Gone!

They had been taken to Los Angeles. Maurice couldn't find them, and neither could he find his personal management or production papers. Streetwise would continue to put out "Candy Girl" and the album; and would continue to do so for a number of years.

But, Maurice Starr had no group. Another door had closed, but this time on his fingers. He was publicly humiliated in Roxbury; and in the music world, scorned and laughed at. The New Edition, who Steven Machat would end up managing and forming a production company around, were forbidden to ever speak Maurice's name again. And, for six long years, never did. They were given new managers and new producers. MCA would go on to sell millions and millions more of the New Edition albums. Maurice would become a recluse in Roxbury, his fingers smashed in the door, trying to ride on The New Edition success by doing productions with groups like Confunction and the Stylistics, but not having any success.

People were thinking that he did the New Edition wrong, and that's why they left him. He was watching them go to the top never telling anybody about what he had done for them. It wasn't exactly back to

The Rise of New Kids on the Block...

Doc's, but Maurice was crushed physically and mentally; and Willie Mae and Ray prayed for him.

Record Producers Tony Rose and Maurice Starr hanging out at the Boston Music Awards with Bobby Brown - 1989.

Year's later, at the Boston Music Awards, Maurice just beginning to know that he was on a spaceship ride to Mars with the New Kids On The Block. They were up to five million "Hangin Tough" albums sold. Bobby Brown took a picture with Maurice—their arms around each other, and spoke for the first time in six years. Bobby told Maurice "I'm glad for you".

Part Four
The Building of an Empire

The Rise of New Kids on the Block...

Chapter Sixteen
The Evolution Begins

And now, boys and girls, let me tell you a story of great significance, of enormous proportions, of major importance.

It's a story filled with dreams, hopes, magic, and more important than anything, FATE!

And, now let me tell you what happened! The real story of Maurice Starr and New Kids on the Block.

Once upon a time............

In 1984 Mary Alford felt like she had been used. Margo had left her for Richard "Dimples" Fields, a popular Southern singer who'd had a huge hit in the seventies called "She's Got Papers On Me" by Dimples. But, most important, in 1984 Dimples had a production deal with RCA Records for distribution of himself and artists he signed to "Dat Richfield Kat (DRK) Productions". Mary had supported Margo, a popular child singer, home-grown in Roxbury raised as Margo Furtado, now one of the hottest—if not the hottest singer on the Roxbury music scene—now known as Margo Thunder (and her two childhood friends Wanda Perry and Leslie Jones) and Entrigue. Mary had supported the group. She'd bought costumes, fed, housed, groomed, provided transportation and rehearsal space for them; brought her white self into Roxbury where she was the only white girl hanging around in Roscoe's, Lane's and Ben's Lounges. She got gigs for her girls, booking them and giving them all the money, plus money she'd make from her job. Even in the early

Roxbury (1980-1983) days people would say "Man, them girls sure treat Mary bad." People liked Mary Alford. Why she would want to manage a black singing group, nobody knew. But, secretly, she loved black music and black people, and by managing (supporting) a black group, she had a chance to hear the music, be down, and be accepted on the black music scene.

Mary made all the parties, all the openings, and hit the clubs regularly every Thursday, Friday and Saturday. She had a black way of talking, wore glasses, pants, jackets (not a trashy type of white girl that likes black street dudes, but a respectable hard-working blue-collar class woman) doing business with you. Mary was accepted and knew everyone worth knowing on the scene. She was liked and respected, and everyone did business with her.

In time, Mary had the hottest act on the scene. Margo, Wanda and Leslie were getting known, traveling out of state, appearing in New York, doing recording dates with everybody in Boston and New York. They simply had the best voices of anybody (then and now) to come from Roxbury, and everybody knew Mary Alford managed Margo Thunder and Entrigue.

In late 1983, the girls lacked just one thing. It seemed that everybody on the Roxbury scene had records out, had record deals, and were making names for themselves. They had even done backup singing for Prince Charles and the City Beat Band, now signed to Virgin Records and touring in Europe and the U.S. behind two top-selling albums. It seemed like everybody had a deal, but them, and they started putting pressure on Mary to get them a recording contract. Mary pushed and brought them to the attention of a newly formed production company in New York. Before you could say "one, two, three", "Dimples" took Margo, Wanda and Leslie to Los Angeles, made them his backup singers, change their name to "9.9", kept them on hold until 1985, and produced an album released on RCA Records called "9.9". They had a moderate radio hit with the single "All Of Me For All Of You" and the album died.

The Evolution Begins

Used up in L.A. and by Dimples, and disgusted with life, they came back to Boston in 1987.

But, in 1984, Mary had felt used, abused, and kicked to the curb, and North Dorchester "working-class girl" mad. Margo and the girls had left her, moved to Los Angeles, and were tearing Hollywood up. In 1984 Mary was still living in Dorchester, riding up and down the same old streets, still working the same old job. Mary on the way to the store riding up American Legion Highway on her way to Zayre's Mall, and Maurice Starr brooding and still in shock (not even able to listen to the radio in fear of a New Edition song coming on), picked the same hour, minute and second to ride up the highway. Maurice spotted Mary, and fate met them head on.

Now, while Maurice and Mary were riding around in Roxbury, Michael Jonzun was out there in the world getting rich and famous as the "Jonzun Crew". He would do two million ("Lost in Space") albums and three million singles for Tom Silverman's Tommy Boy Records, making enough money to move out of 20 Linwood Square, purchase a home in Westwood Massachusetts, get a Mercedes-Benz, and buy a fully loaded 24-track recording studio, already established in business, on Boylston Street near downtown Boston. The studio would now be called "Mission Control".

Usually Maurice and Michael had shared songwriting and production credits, but once Michael had signed with Tom, Tom became his co-producer and cut Maurice out from the money made on the albums. It wasn't Michael's fault. That was a condition of Michael's being signed to Tommy Boy Records. Michael would roll his eyes whenever Tom was mentioned as his co-producer. So, in 1984 Maurice, Michael and the Johnson Brothers owned their own 24-track recording studio, which was bought through Michael's success, and if Maurice didn't actually own it, well, baby brother Michael wasn't adverse to giving free studio time to Maurice and the rest of his brothers. Hey! To help them out. Besides Willie Mae would have come up from Florida and hit him over the head, if he hadn't.

103

While brooding at 20 Linwood Square over the loss of the New Edition, Maurice started remembering a group that came out of Utah, who gave the Jackson Five a run for their money, a run for their vast teenage market. The group was the Osmond Brothers, Similar in musical orientation and upbringing to the Jackson Five and the Johnson Brothers, except they were white. The Osmonds were a white pop singing group that took over a world of young white screaming pre-teen and teenage girls, and after a few years, left a void—a hole in their sweet young hearts—much as the Jackson Five had done (up until the arrival of "The New Edition") to the hearts of young sweet black girls.

As Maurice would say, years later, "Given the demographics of the country and the history of the music business, I figured that five white kids could be very big. If New Edition was as big as they were, I could imagine what would happen if white kids were doing the same thing." But where to find them? Maurice continues, "What I had in mind for New Edition was making them the new Jackson Five? With New Kids, I wanted to re-create the Osmonds…The Osmonds had talent, but they didn't have soul, and they didn't have enough good material. The New Kids are different from the Osmonds. They have talent and soul and good material—good black material".

Chapter Seventeen
The Search Is On

"I was looking for kids with looks, charisma and determination, kids with soul", said Maurice. "I needed kids who Knew the black culture—white kids who were hip enough to hang with blacks. But, where to find them?"

Boston, at best, was a racially divided city. Like most cities in the United States, blacks did not visit whites and whites did not visit blacks on a visit made up of friendship (not political or business, but socially) because they wanted to be friends. You would have to grow up together with each other for that to happen. And, Maurice didn't know anybody that had grown up with white kids.

So, in 1984 when Maurice literally ran into Mary Alford—talent scout, manager, and resident of North Dorchester—some half-formed ideas clicked into place. "Mary was white, and lived with white people. Mary also had black awareness, and got along excellently with black people. Thus, where Mary lived, there must be other white people like her." It was almost magical because Mary had also been thinking of putting together a cute white singing group that would have a black sound.

Now, Maurice had never stopped writing and recording songs. Brother Michael had left the eight-track recording equipment at 20 Linwood Square, and Maurice took full advantage of it. No! Songs were not Maurice's most pressing problem at all. Songs, tapes, cassettes, 1/4" tapes, ½" tapes and musical instruments were all over the place—in his bedroom, the studio, downstairs, upstairs. Tapes and cassettes would fall out of the closets when you opened the doors. There'd be so many of them…all kinds of tapes and songs …but, no piece of paper with Ralph's, Bobby's, Ronnie's, Michael's, Ricky's, and their mothers' and fathers' names on it; meaning Maurice couldn't find a legal contract giving him power-of-attorney over the New Edition name and management of the group.

He could find tapes, but he couldn't find that piece of paper. Maurice went to court anyway, with Mark Weiner leading the way for four years. In 1987, the courts awarded New Edition their name, but they had to pay Maurice Starr, Streetwise Records and Boston International Records $100,000 (dollars). Maurice had lost, but in truth, they all had lost—all except the lawyers, Steven Machet and MCA. The New Edition saw all the money they had earned go to the management company and lawyers, and Maurice never expected anything. He had sued because in God's eyes he was right, and God looked out for him. God did.

By the time the suit was ended, the New Kids on the Block had a record deal. Yes, Maurice had the music—music he had sitting there—written with Ralph, Ronnie, Ricky, Michael and Bobby in mind. Music with five part harmony was sitting there, waiting for some young male voices to sing to some sweet, fine, young girls.

Soon after they met, Maurice and Mary got together (the music man and the manager). Mary now had a goal, a chance, to redeem herself. She knew Maurice's' capabilities, knew that if she found the right kids, Maurice would do the job. Night and day, day and night, she thought of nothing else. Her main thought was to put together a dream group - the pop equivalent of New Edition. Together, Mary Alford and Maurice Starr, both victimized by black groups, which were too greedy to be loyal, would put together a group where love and loyalty would come first. It would be a group that they could give all their dedication and experience to, a group they would train and teach (from A to Z) the fundaments—the basics of music and show business.

The New Kids perform live.

The Rise of New Kids on the Block...

Mary put ads in all the Boston music publications. She went to North Dorchester and asked all the girls in her neighborhood if they knew of any cute guys who could sing, dance, or play instruments. Maurice held talent shows at the Lee School and at Roscoe's. The main qualities that Maurice and Mary were looking for were: 1) They had to have unique personalities; 2) They had to be able to rap, dance and Sing; 3) They had to be under eighteen years of age; 4) They had to be white.

Donnie Wahlberg—fifteen years old—into Michael Jackson rap, dancing, going to school with black kids and talent shows, outgoing, tough, a drummer, smart, street-hip, had heard about Maurice Starr because of New Edition. They were the big talk in all the Roxbury schools. Donnie also heard the producer of New Edition was looking for white kids to form a group. He was interested. Donnie was a rapper, not a singer. He could rap, dance, jump around, was heavy on personality and the black culture.

Maurice says, "they had to have some sort of gimmick, then we could build the talent as time went on. In the beginning, the guys didn't have to be the greatest singers in the world, but they needed an attitude and a look."

Mary put the word out, and Donnie responded. He auditioned for Maurice and Mary doing impersonations of Michael Jackson, moonwalking and dancing. He told Maurice he couldn't sing, and Maurice told Donnie that it didn't matter, he could teach him. Donnie said later, "We're very close to Maurice, he's been a very good teacher. I know when I started out, I had never sung before. I was scared, but Maurice gave me confidence. He built me up. He built us all up. He made us feel like we could do anything. His confidence in us has been incredible. Without it, I don't think we could have made it."

Maurice, living at 20 Linwood Square, with memories of the old Johnson Brothers Band and New Edition would soon move to a new home in Roxbury, across the street from a landmark church, but still smack in the middle of the ghetto. 27 Dudley Street was a shell—a condemned building—huge, with great possibilities. But, the best thing was that the price was right — $27,500. And, Calvin, Elvin and Donnie Johnson had nothing but time, to fix up Maurice's house—the house that Donnie, Jordan, Jonathan, Danny and Joey would practically grow up in.

Maurice signed Donnie. This time, there would be no fooling around with contracts. Parents would have to sign, with court approval, and both sides would use lawyers—attorney Mark Weiner for Maurice Starr, and attorney Barry Rosenthal of Lewin and Rosenthal for the group. Maurice said of Donnie, "You could tell right away he was a genius. I asked him if he could Rap, and he went on non-stop. He had a cool walk and a cool talk. It was beautiful."

Maurice and Mary asked Donnie if he had any friends. Now Danny was into track and break dancing, and didn't know if he wanted to give something like that his complete dedication. But Jordan said "yes" when Donnie called him. Jordan auditioned for Maurice and Mary, and remembers that Maurice told him to get ready to be great. "You are going to be the biggest thing in the world." Jordan told him that he just wanted a scooter. Jordan also told Maurice and Mary that he had a brother who could sing. This made them very happy because they knew that two kids who had grown up singing, like Jordan and Jonathan had in their school and in church, were invaluable.

Soon after, Danny came to Roxbury and joined up. Donnie's brother Mark Wahlberg was in the original group, but decided that the pace might not be what he wanted, and his parents felt that he might be a little young. An even sadder story was that the parents of Jamie Kelly, a very good friend of Donnie's, and a member of the group (until racial prejudice reared it's head), and Jamie's parents—more in line with the South Boston mentality—came up with an excuse to pull Jamie out of the group.

The Rise of New Kids on the Block...

On February 15th, 1985 Mary picked up Joe McIntyre. Joey remembers that day well. "Mary picked me up and I was really scared. I went to Maurice Starr's house, and tried out. I sang one of the songs that the group was about to record, and afterwards we got into the car, and Mary asked me 'well, do you want to be in the group? You've got the part'." Joey also sang Nat King Cole's song "Love". Donnie, Jordan Jonathan and Danny had been amateurs when the group was formed, but young Joey, at twelve, was a seasoned professional, and with Joey, Maurice would have an operatic voice (a high kid voice).

Chapter Eighteen
Hard Work Prevails

And now, he had the perfect group—a rapper, a choirboy, a singer, a dancer and an actor. But, with training in the Maurice Starr School of Music they would do everything as one.

Maurice, at first, called them Nynuk—as in "Nynuk of the North", and embarked them The Maurice Starr School of Music Appreciation: listening to rap and black music—really listening. They learned how to hear and have a certain tone while singing, when to open

and close their mouths, when to sing and not to sing vibrato. Maurice put them with black choreographer David Vaughan, a young black kid from Dorchester who probably was one of the anticipators and originators of breakdancing and line techno-lock dancing, and later Tyrone Procter, a well-known black national choreographer.

Maurice would write new songs, and the group would take the cassettes to the Lee School in Dorchester and rehearse in front of black kids. Maurice says "I put the group there to see the black talent, to feel the vibe. That's where the New Kids learned dancing and singing. You can be black, and not be convincing, but to be white, you have to be 1000 times more convincing, so it was work. I made sure they made the right moves. I wanted regular guys, so they dressed themselves, but I put them with the right type of people."

And, work they did. Those boys worked hard in school and under Maurice's' guidance and tutelage, giving Maurice and Mary their belief back…their confidence back. Donnie, Jordan, Jonathan, Danny and Joey would rehearse over Jordan and Jonathan's. Mother Marlene remembers them "The first years when they were trying to get it all together…they rehearsed regularly in my basement. I would hear my boys… fighting like cats and dogs with each other. I thought—this group is going to tear my kids apart. Jordan had had all this breakdancing experience. He could move more naturally. Jonathan really, really struggled to loosen up so he could do those dance steps. Jordan was doing some of the choreography, and would expect Jon to immediately do it. He knew that some people could not do it as easily as he could. He wanted it to happen quickly… when Jon would forget a step, because it was not natural to Jon, Jordan would get annoyed. Then when rehearsal would be over, it would be like nothing happened. So, I really had to look at that and say, 'Okay, mother, back off don't get upset. They are going to do their fighting. That is how they are going to release their tension doing this thing.' And pretty soon, rehearsal, watching, listening and learning started becoming natural to all five, and they started to move as one."

Hard Work Prevails

Pretty soon, they were playing the black clubs in Roxbury—Roscoes, Vern's, Corteez—the Strand Theater, Maurice's Hollywood Talent Night and talent shows at the Lee School. And, real soon, all the kids knew who they were. They got used to seeing them around. The black kids at school, the black people at the clubs and the Roxbury music scene saw Maurice's latest discovery. Some people (hey, a lot of people) laughed, thought they were funny and couldn't dance. But, Maurice pushed them. "Maurice has been like a father to us", Jon said. "He's been our biggest influence." Maurice also encouraged the New Kids to learn to play instruments and taught the group how to write and produce their own songs, and opened up a new horizon for them.

The New Kids' parents were very concerned about their boys, not because Maurice was black and a lot of their work was done in Roxbury, but they wondered if the boys could handle their school work and home life. Alma, Donnie's mother, spoke for all the parents when she said "I was scared. I really wanted Donnie to finish his schooling; I was afraid that might get pushed aside, so I was a little nervous about that. I was also nervous about him being away from home, being with people that I didn't know. I wanted to be very involved, so I went to every rehearsal, every neighborhood show, every time they performed. I was there until I started to feel secure about the people he was dealing with. They really cared about him, and Donnie proved to me that he could do his schooling, sing with the group and have a part-time job. He did well at all three.

The parents all had long talks with Maurice, and he impressed them with his sincerity, his inner belief, his faith and his musical genius. Maurice and Mary were now ready to take Nynuk to the second stage.... Dick Scott had retained his ties with Maurice, and although he was not entirely in the music business industry, he still had plenty of contacts in the upper echelons of the record companies through his work with the United Cerebral Palsy Foundation, and Maurice gave Dick a four song demo-tape, which he had produced at his house.

Erik Nuri, a black New Yorker who had graduated from Harvard University, adopted Boston, and was influenced by Boston's political and music scene. He was known to most people in Roxbury where he lived as a sax player and head of a record company called Beantown Records (owned by Lymon Underwood, heir to the Underwood Devil Ham fortune). Around 1984, through mismanagement, Beantown folded, and Erik Nuri left for New York and Los Angeles, where he landed a job in the A & R Department at CBS Records, and became a protégé of the legendary record company executive Larkin Arnold. Larkin's ear for music had resulted in over 40 million records sold for the various companies he worked for. Larkin, a Vice President of CBS Records was one of four black record company executives able to write a check for one million dollars or more to an artist or company. At CBS, Larkin had a counterpart named Cecil Holmes, a very formidable record company Executive who was one of the four.

So, Maurice, Mary and Dick began shopping their tape….the only executives that would talk to them were black, and they thought the idea of a white kid group singing black music had to be a joke. Eric Nuri was a sax player, more inclined to be on the jazz scene in Boston, and as head of the Black Caucus, he had strong political ties, and used them well. In 1979, he was also one of a handful of black entrepreneurs to release a record on his own label. "Let's Vote" was a political rap—one of the first of its kind—and gave Erik credibility with the Roxbury scene. A performer with his own jazz band, he knew Maurice and the whole Roxbury scene. Erik wasn't gritty or street smart. He was more inclined to back-room and inner-office deals. Life was very political, very calculating and analytic for Erik. In 1989, divorced from his first wife, he would marry Cheryl Sutton, daughter of Percy Sutton, former Manhattan Borough President and Chairman of Inner City Broadcasting Company. Mr. Sutton was a major stockholder in numerous radio stations, the world famous Apollo Theater, and an Independent Record Company (Apollo Records) distributed by Motown Records.

Chapter Nineteen
Getting In The Door

But in 1985, Erik Nuri was just working his way up, and had been offered a position with CBS Records. Brought in by Larkin Arnold, Erik had some power, and could get a deal signed if Larkin approved. So, now boys and girls, here's how The New Kids got in the door:

The kids have been well rehearsed. They've got a show—dancing and singing to the four new songs. They can audition. The Kids, Maurice believes are ready. Maurice Starr gives the tape to Erik Nuri. Erik new of Maurice's immense talent and the real story of who groomed the New Edition, because he was in Boston during their rise. Erik believed in Maurice and believed Maurice would deliver the goods. Larkin Arnold listened to Erik.

Meanwhile, Mary's booking Nynuk—anywhere and everywhere—playing Harlem, anywhere they could put them on the bill, but sill no deal. Nobody thought it would work. At a show in Boston called the "Kite Festival", held in Roxbury's Franklin Park, an audience of 10,000 black kids booed and threw rocks at them. Donnie, the tough guy, had to be dragged off the stage. He wouldn't stop performing, even after he was hit a few times with cans.

Danny explains "…When we started out, we did most of our shows in black neighborhoods because our producer felt that if we could perform in front of black audiences, and get over, we could go anywhere and get over, because we had to be so much better to get over in black neighborhoods than in white neighborhoods where they'd accept us easier."

The show consisted then, as it does now, of their five-part harmony, including: Donnie's rap influence, Jordan's sweet enchanting voice, Joey's cute high lilt, and Danny and Jonathan's mid-range masculinity. There was lots of dancing and crowd involvement. Soon, Erik was able to convince Larkin to audition the group. The happiest day, up to that point, in Donnie's, Jordan's, Jonathan's, Danny's, and Joey's lives was when Maurice, Mary and Dick told them CBS was going to release one of the songs that Maurice had written and produced. Erik had brought them in. The deal was CBS would release "Be My Girl" an infectious "bubble gum pop" song. If the single sold well enough, an album deal was promised.

The deal was cut in January 1986, and "Be My Girl" was released in April 1986, and Mary, Dick and Maurice went to work. Dick used his considerable influence with United Cerebral Palsy events, and the Kids began doing telethons and appearances for various fundraisers. On July 4th, they performed at the Statue of Liberty before 3,000 people. They opened up shows for Lisa Lisa and the Cult Jam; and the Four Tops. As Donnie says "We were known in black parts of town, but not in the white parts. We played a lot of ghetto places. We played Harlem. We did the Apollo Theater. We played some tough places". It was a family situation, with Mary hustling around providing transportation, getting the kids to and from dates, Dick and Mary setting up the next performances, and interviews.

The teen magazines were beginning to identify with the boys. Subsequently, New Kids on the Block would become the most photographed and written-about celebrities in history. But, for now, an interview in "Teen Beat" was just great. The Kids loved it, and loved it even more, when Maurice told them he was changing the name from Nynuk to the New Kids on the Block. "New Kids on the Block" was the name of a rap song that Donnie and Maurice had written that would show up later on the first album.

Getting In The Door

With all the push the team did "Be My Girl" was a disappointment—a big one. It did not sell close to what a company like CBS Records thought it should. A respectable number would have been 50,000 sales.

But Maurice Starr knew one important thing—that singing groups might be a "dime a dozen". There might be millions of singing groups in the United States, hundreds of thousands of people singing, rapping and dancing; but, there was only white group in the whole entire world ready to be black—ready to fill that void in those sweet young girls' hearts. They were ready to dance for them, sing and sweat for them, and give them the hardest-working man-in-showbusiness routine. They knew about the funk and sweat of James Brown and the Johnson Brothers, and Maurice knew he had it! He was living it. It was his party, and you were all invited to come see and hear the New Kids on the Block.

Later, Maurice would say in an interview, "They have white skins, but they're black...they have soul. They sing black. That's how I taught them to sing." Something else Maurice noted, makes the

The Rise of New Kids on the Block...

New Kids different. "They have me as a manager". He laughs, and says "A hit teen white group, managed by a black man, a black man who also writes, produces and arranges their albums, who also created the group. That just doesn't happen in this business."

....Yeah, boy! Maurice knew for a fact that he had something different, and he persuaded Larkin Arnold and Erik Nuri to overlook the single sales, and to give him a budget to produce an album. The record executives went for the idea, and decided to record an album. The album, released in late 1986, was recorded at Michael Jonzun's studio "Mission Control"; and various other New England locations. Maurice Starr played drums, bass and lead guitar, vocorder, piano, strings, Juno 60, DX-7, mini Moog, OBX, emulator and lots of funk black culture. Other players were: Jimmy Johnson—congo on "Stop It Girl" and Popsicle", Gordon Worthy—additional keyboards on "Treat Me Right" and "Be My Girl"; and Mark Fantani—guitar solo on "Stop It Girl". Maurice Starr played and programmed the Linn, Roland and DMX drum machines. Maurice wrote and produced the entire album, co-writing two tunes, and Erik Nuri, getting co-writing credit on another song. Donnie Wahlberg would be involved in the writing of two songs—one with Maurice, and one with Erik Nuri.

Side one featured: "Stop It Girl" (M. Starr), "Didn't I (Blow Your Mind)" (W.Hart/T.Bell), "Popsicle" (M. Starr), "Angel" (M. Starr/J. Appra), "Be My Girl" (M. Starr); side two: "New Kids on the Block" (M. Starr/D. Wahlberg), "Are You Down" (A.J./E. Nuri/K. Banki/ D. Wahlberg), "I Wanna Be Loved by You" (M. Starr), "Don't Give Up On Me" (M. Starr), and "Treat me Right" (M. Starr). The album is dedicated to "Our wonderful mothers, and the mother of Maurice Starr—Mrs. Willie Mae Johnson". Special thanks to "God"; Mary Alford—for her guidance; Maurice Starr - for his music and making us his #1; and our parents—for their support. The album was produced by Maurice Starr for Maurice Starr Productions, Inc.; written and arranged by Maurice Starr for Maurice Starr Productions, and Big Step Productions Inc. (except for "Didn't

I (Blow Your Mind)" and "Are You Down". Managed and directed exclusively by Big Step Management, Inc.; Mary Alford, personal manager; Dick Scott, General manager. Executive Producers—Larkin Arnold and Erik Nuri.

The New Kids on the Block had their first album out. Two more singles followed, "Stop It Girl" and "Didn't I (Blow Your Mind)". Again, the New Kids hit the road. They started appearing in as many teen magazines as possible. Donnie tells it "anyone who says we didn't earn what we've got now, should have been with us then. We were sleeping in cheap motels, and we were always on the road, always talking to fans, doing as many radio shows as possible." They were carrying around their backing tape, dancing and singing on stage to taped material because they couldn't afford a band. Night after night, they were on a mission to succeed. They would not give up, nor would they be disloyal to Maurice. It was hard work, but Maurice loved those kids…and they knew it.

The album was a mixture of soul, R & B, and hip-hop. It was bubble-gum music, cute, but not for the urban black audience that CBS was trying to sell them to. CBS was trying to sell them to a black audience, hoping they would crossover to a white audience, and black radio programmers had resisted. Maurice hit the road, went to all the black radio stations—records in his hands, just like the old days—but, only a few of his real friends, like Elroy R.C. Smith (then at W.I.L.D. in Boston) and Steve Crumbley (in Virginia) responded. Pretty soon, in 1987, the kids knew this album was not going to be the success that they had hoped it would be. Donnie said, "I think the first record failing was good for us. We tasted failure, and maybe learned how to avoid it."

All the tiny clubs and social halls, the photo sessions and in-store record signings had not helped the sales of "New Kids on the Block". The first album was bombing, and there was nothing that Dick Scott, Mary Alford or Maurice Starr could do about it. The album sold under 20,000 copies. Eventually, Erik Nuri lost his job at CBS Records, and things looked dismal for the group. But,

Maurice had seen harder, and let the boys know that this wasn't the end of the world. They could still do it.

He went back to CBS Records, still believing, still fanatical, and convinced Cecil Holmes (Vice President of CBS) to give him one more shot, one more chance. He would bring home a hit….he knew he could. Besides, the groundwork had been laid. Almost every day, the New Kids were doing interviews or track-dates somewhere. They could get a following, find a market…somewhere. Maurice believed. In fact, the Kid's parents believed. They saw it in his eyes, and heard it when he spoke. Maurice was on a mission to Mars, and nothing or nobody could tell him this was not going to be the greatest group in the world.

Chapter Twenty
Fate Takes An Upper Hand

Well, Cecil believed one more time. In the meantime, Dick Scott tightened up contracts, incorporating everything in sight, tying everything down…iron-clad contracts. Maurice had told him, this time, this was it. His mother in Florida, Willie Mae, had had a dream; and this next album was going to be the biggest thing in the world.

Meanwhile, for Donnie, Jordan, Jonathan, Danny and Joey, life continued as usual… well, not so usual. After all, they were a select breed on the Roxbury scene. They'd had a few singles and an album out. They had heard their voices coming over loud and clear on the radio, done a lot of traveling, spent time in New York hanging out at the CBS "Black Rock" Record headquarters, had met and been introduced to some important people around the country, had been seen on T.V. by themselves, and all the rest of the boys and girls that had gone to schools with them in Roxbury and Boston (especially the girls). They were major celebrities, playing in a small playground.

Hey! How many other kids had their own record deal and were being produced by Maurice Starr? Some of the kids were jealous, and a lot of the people were upset because they were wondering why Maurice was putting so much of his efforts and time into white boys. But, they didn't know the pain that Maurice had gone through during the New Edition period. They didn't know how some in Roxbury had turned their backs on him—the politicians, the business community, the entertainment community. They had proven how shallow and closed-minded they were. They didn't know that failure in the music business was as common as getting a glass of water…failure, one day…gold records and multi-million dollar status, the next. Talent was unpredictable. If you had it, you had it, and if you were patient enough, it would show up and give you the big prize. No, a lot of people didn't know about patience, but Maurice did, and he had a long memory. Again Roxbury had failed him while he was trying to do something positive with the New Kids on the Block, running around with their records. He encountered a lot of hostility because the kids were white. Maurice was laughed at and talked about, sometimes to his face, most of the time behind his back. He would never forget this.

Oh, Maurice did have his admirers and special friends in Roxbury—people who loved him—loved him for his brilliance, his special way of making you feel good (like you knew you were in the presence of someone special). Maurice was the type of guy who would put some hominy grits on, and that would make you feel right at home, but, mainly people loved Maurice because he was a sweet guy. He'd give you the shirt off his back talking, laughing, mimicking everybody in sight. He was a sight to behold—him and his white group, and them boys loved him, like there was no tomorrow. Yeah, Maurice had a long memory. His motto was "don't get mad, get even". He would never really feel good about the leadership of Roxbury—the politicians and business people—and , they would not be included in the success of New Kids.

Chapter Twenty-One
The Struggle Continues

Upon leaving Tommy Boy Records, Michael Jonzun signed with A & M Records. He upgraded his recording studio "Mission Control" by adding a SSL (Solid State Logic) 24-track board. He then redeemed himself in Maurice's eyes by selling him his Mission Control's old console board and tape deck for $20,000– a bargain—and with the family way of doing things, of course Maurice wouldn't have to pay for it all at once. They were brothers, but it was business and some payments would have to be made. This one act of brotherly kindness would put the final click in Maurice Starr's and The New Kids on the Block's rise to fame.

Maurice Starr, again, through the success of Michael, had what he had been needing all along—a twenty-four track recording studio console, tape deck (24 tracks), effects units, compressor, the works—a complete recording studio. Maurice could record to his heart's content—24 hours a day, everyday, any time during the day, all day and night, always and anytime. He could take his time, get the music down right, re-work it, re-sing it, re-edit it, re-mix it, and mix some more, lay down the tracks just right—no mistakes recording.

He would spend the entire year working on the songs, listening to music on the radio, humming to himself in bed, hearing and getting plenty of feedback from Donnie, Jordan and Danny, who were getting their own feedback from their black friends at school, who were making suggestions to them on how to have a better album next time. These black friends gave them records and sang with the New

Kids, rapped with them, worked with them on beats and drum machines. They showed them what was new, what was fresh, how to talk, how to walk, how to live black. Yeah boy! The New Kids had some good friends, and when they were New Kids on the Block—rich and famous—they would come back home to Roxbury, Dorchester and North Dorchester, and try to help some of those friends out (get them a record deal).

The New Kids would bring back this information to Maurice, who would then translate it into the language of music. As good a teacher as Maurice was, he was as good a listener, and he listened, watched and saw well. The whole of 1987, Maurice watched MTV, BET, (all the video shows) soaking up information like a sponge. The New Kids went to school. Some, like Donnie (who kept a part-time job as a shoe clerk) worked part-time. Late afternoons they'd all congregate over at Maurice's house, everyday, to work on songs, rehearse the newest dance steps, and learn how to play music as an assembled band. Donnie was on drums, Jordan on keyboard, Jonathan picking up the sax, Danny learning the bass guitar and little Joe playing tambourines. And, slowly, what at first was noise, began to sound like music through constant rehearsing, constant practice at Maurice's and at home. All day, every day, these boys worked hard - the Johnson brothers' way—hard practice and lots of group teamwork and belief, and pretty soon the New Kids on the Block were becoming a unit, moving as one.

It was showing up on the tape and in the studio. Their voices were becoming more musical. It was coming through loud and clear, right over the electronics, coming out of the speakers. All the hard work was paying off. The New Kids on the Block had a sound, they were musical…and Maurice told everybody, everybody he met… like he had dreamed it, like God or his mother had given him a message "The New Kids On the Block Are Going To Be the Biggest Act In The World!" It was loud and clear, for everyone to hear. He told this over and over to the boys. They believed him, their parents believed, Mary Alford believed, Dick Scott believed, anybody who really knew and loved Maurice believed...at least believed that something big was going to happen.

During this period, Maurice could also be found engineering and producing music for other people—some professional, some amateur. Some people wouldn't even know that the guy plugging in the chords, turning knobs, putting the tape on, and coaching their voices was the famous Maurice Starr. Maurice would continue working for hire, up until March 1988. Some people (when they think about it) must say "Wow! that's the guy who engineered my recording!"

Elvin was busy doing construction, setting up his own business, and doing work on Maurice's house. Sonny would help out from time to time, and Calvin was drinking plenty of Budweiser's, cooking great meals, keeping the kids fed on a daily basis, keeping the house clean (along with Phaedra Butler, an aspiring young singer who Maurice had been living with for two years). Maurice had recorded some songs on her as Phaedra and the Body Construction, secured a small deal with Capital Records, and was in love...Maurice took Phaedra everywhere with him.

In 1988 Maurice turned the tapes over to Cecil Holmes at CBS Records, and "Please Don't Go Girl" was picked as the first release. Again, Maurice had turned chords around, taking from a classic Jackson Five song, and was now on the verge of turning his song into a classic. "Please Don't Go Girl" came out in February 1988. Elroy R.C. Smith, then still Programming Director at WILD Radio (Boston) jumped on it right away. This record had the smooth mix of soul and R & B music, and was just right for black radio.

By now most black radio programmers across the country knew that New Kids On The Block were a white group, and were creating their own form of backlash—not playing it because they were white. The same thing was true of black publications, who said, "let the white magazines run their stories." The CBS Promotion team was having a hard time with black media. But, Maurice would do something very smart, taking some advice from a friend who was going to put out a video on a group that they had produced together independently. Maurice decided to do a video on New Kids on the Block himself. There was just one catch. Maurice, Mary, Dick, The New Kids, their parents and the Johnson Brothers had no money... at least not enough money to produce a video.

Chapter Twenty-Two
Taking A Stand

So, Maurice called the only people in the world he knew, without a doubt, would give up everything they had—every thing they owned, whose belief and guidance had been with him and his brothers always, from the beginning. He called Ray, Sr. and Willie Mae Johnson—his parents. Willie Mae sent $15,000, Maurice hired a director, found a video production crew; and the rest, well… "It launched their careers", cred its Starr, "and, not only did my mother write it, she paid for it, financed it, because at the time, I couldn't." Willie Mae John son, after all those years, had not only put up her love and belief, but the money, along with some money from good ole Roscoe Gorham who was now in the Goodyear Tire Business. That move would cement the group on a national basis; because in less than a month after the production was finished, "Please Don't Go Girl" was doing heavy rotation on MTV and BET.

All across the nation, without ever leaving home, they were beginning to be known. Things were starting to happen. Donnie, Danny, Jordan, Jon a than and Joe were becoming media stars. You could turn the TV on, and see them all the time. The video Maurice had produced with his mother's script and financing was a hit—a monstrous hit. With out leaving home, New Kids on the Block were a success, but not a Billboard charting success. The album had been released without any fanfare, and the single was sinking fast.

Writer's Note: Upon the advice of Tony Rose, Maurice decided to do a video on New Kids on the Block's single, "Please Don't Go Girl."

Maurice, at home, decided to concentrate and put some time into Phaedra Butler's career. Learning that Margo Thunder was back in

Boston, he arranged for Margo Thunder to come to his studio (called House of Hits) and record. She would do some background work with Phaedra. Margo was also looking to put together a new group to try to get another recording contract. That night Maurice went to bed early. The next morning, he learned that the giggles and laughter between Phaedra and Margo had a double meaning, because Phaedra was gone with Margo. During the next few weeks, Phaedra would tell Maurice how she hated him, was only using him to get a record deal and a record out, and he hadn't even done that. Coached by Margo, Phaedra was doing a job on Maurice's sanity. His concentration was off the record and on Phaedra. He ripped his studio apart and wouldn't come out of his room. He loved Phaedra, and now it was over. But, with a friend's help, he got back on track, started watching TV...BET and all. Maurice got inspired. It was a shame, because Phaedra had less than eight months to go before she would have been on the "good ship lollipop".

Sure! The video success was inspiring, and Maurice, Mary and Dick got the New Kids back on the road, back to playing two or three different clubs a night, lip syncing with their cassette tape of music (since they still couldn't afford a band) playing county and state fairs, nightclubs from Tijuana, Mexico to Boston, Massachusetts. It was the same route as before, but somehow it felt different. It was the video. More people knew about them, had seen them. All over—from Nevada to Oregon, from Albuquerque to South Carolina—girls were checking this out. They were different. They were white, but they were singing, dancing, acting black. The mall girls across the United States had never seen anything like this.

This underused market of untapped millions was sitting there for someone to scratch their libidos—to fill that hole in their hearts. These pre-teen and teenage girls were, by word-of-mouth and that video, finding the New Kids On The Block and liking what they saw. Clean, funky, enchanting, athletic and smooth; spelled Joey, Donnie, Jordan, Danny and Jonathan. The girls had never seen anything like them in their lives...and they looked just like them! In

Taking A Stand

one minute, the New Kids On the Block were going to have ten million girlfriends. Yeah! Maurice knew about it! He was out there on the road, seeing it happen, watching the girls' responses. Oh, he knew, but how to tell and convince CBS. It wasn't showing up on sales charts or radio play charts. Black kids weren't buying it, and the white kids weren't hearing it on the radio at all.

Hal Jackson, in all probability, was the greatest radio programmer ever in the history of radio. He was a man known for building radio stations, and bringing them into The #1 spot on the Arbitron Ratings in whichever market he was in. Hal was also a founder and the architect of the enormous success of the Inner City Broad casting Corporation that included the Power House New York radio base WBLS—The House That Hal Jackson Built and Format ted, and that Frankie Crocker sat in. Hal Jackson was, quite simply, one of the baddest" cats in all of American Music History. He knew, and was on speaking terms with everyone in the recording industry, walked hand-in-hand with all its Crown Princes and Princesses.

Hal had been around since the thirties. He had dined with Franklin Delano Roosevelt at the White House. Hal is a great, great man and a sweet guy, who'd help anybody and everybody, give you a break, see what you could do with it. Hal also had access to the world famous Apollo Theatre in Harlem on 125th Street. After all, he was the Group Chairman of Inner City Broad casting Corporation and they owned the Apollo Theatre, and counted among his many friends Tony and Yvonne Rose who were also, at that time in 1988, the directors of the Hal Jack son's Talented Teen Competition in Rhode Island.

Writer's Note: I called Hal Jackson at WBLS-Radio in New York City and asked if he would meet with Maurice Starr and New Kids on the Block. He said 'yes' and I told Maurice that I had spoken to Hal Jackson, and he should go see Hal at his Madison Avenue office.

Maurice Starr rode up in the elevator to the twenty-second floor, with Donnie, Jordan, Jonathan, Danny and Joe. Confident, talking

The Rise of New Kids on the Block...

big, letting the boys know he was right there. The boys, loving it, were rehearsed and ready. They had better be! It was June 1988 and they were just about to break down the door, barge in without an appointment, and see Hal Jackson in his offices at Inner City, home of the biggest and hippest radio station in New York City (four million listeners every day). He would tell his good friends, Tony and Yvonne who had told Maurice to go down and see Hal, that they were right...Maurice and the New Kids came into his office singing and dancing...these kids had something.

They pushed his table and chairs out of the way and performed their way right into Hal Jackson's heart. He loved them. There were white, but they were all right.

After their "audition" with Hal, arrangements were made for the New Kids to appear at the Apollo Theater, and WBLS and the other affiliated Inner City Radio Stations in San Antonio, Detroit and California would boost their radio play of the New Kids on The Block single and their album "Hangin Tough". In June 1988, the Apollo Theater was filled with the toughest audience anywhere in the world. 99.9 percent black, mostly residents of Harlem, they didn't fool around when it came to acts. If the audience didn't like you, they booed you until you voluntarily left their eye sight, or were chased off by a funky clown with a stick. Five white boys, sitting back stage in the dressing room, waited for sure death.

But, the boys were secure in the love and the confidence generated by the people around them. They knew their act backwards and forwards, had been to black schools all their lives, were funkafied by Maurice Starr, and they were tough.... I mean tough kids. They had built up an inner peace, with a hard exterior—Roxbury and North Dorchester tough. They were ready, and they couldn't be beat. For Donnie, Danny, Jordan, Jonathan and Joe, this night would be the greatest night of their careers. Then and now, a fitting climax to their hard work, a sea full of rainbow colored black people, a house full (1,500 strong), all the talent shows, clubs, Lee School shows and little black crowds that Maurice had put them in front of, all would come together in this one night.

And the Apollo crowd loved them—loved their dancing, their singing. They loved them, they cried for them sweet sweet white boys, them young boys, they knew how hard they had to work to be just like them, and how much they had to love black people—the black culture—to want to work that hard. The Apollo roof trembled with applause, again and again. The Kids got two standing ovations and brought the house down. It was an historic moment... never again would the New Kids on the Block play before a sol idly black audience like the Apollo. In two months, they would be dis covered by white America, and leave their roots behind, their black roots behind...eco nomically, but never in spirit.

The Rise of New Kids on the Block...

Chapter Twenty-Three
A Step Closer

But, in June 1988 they had black America Harlem USA on their side…thanks to Hal Jackson.

Top forty radio still excluded the kids, and Maurice was searching for a way to crack it. There was a whisper in Maurice's and Dick's ears that $100,000 might do it. But how? Maurice didn't have it; neither did Dick or Mary. At CBS, the powerful Pop Promotional Department was unwilling to spend the necessary money needed for advertising and radio promotion. The black promotional department was doing all it could, but had limited spending powers. Maurice was at a stand-still. Where to get $100,000?

A Jewish fellow whose great grandfather, grandfather, father and himself had been doing business in Boston since 1901, was in the business of lending money (not Illegally). He had set up a mortgage lending company, using money his family had made in the piano, music school, and real estate business. J.D. Furst was his name, and with a twinkle in his eye, said, "money is my game." A multi-millionaire, J.D. (as he liked to be called), or Jeffrey Furst lived life with a telephone attached to his ear. Limousines—Rolls Royces and Jaguars—he liked to lease or rent to his friends. Lived in Brookline with his wife and two kids, and genuinely liked working with and doing business with black people. He liked to tell everybody he was born in Roxbury.

To Jeffrey, all people were green, the color of money. You either had some money, or wanted to get some money. Jeffrey had been given piano lessons, taught by the world-famous composer Leonard Bernstein, and he knew his way around a piano pretty well. During his twenties, he had been involved in a few music publishing and songwriting ventures—nothing profitable. All Jefftrey's profit came from his every day business concerns; and he was looking to get into the entertainment business in a big way.

Larry Woo and Gordon Worthy (Maurice's cousin) had a production deal with Atlantic Records for a girl singing group called Picture Perfect. Jeffrey was interested, and offered a sizeable amount of money to get involved. But, Larry felt the cost of his independence would be too high, and refused. Soon after, Larry Woo, knowing of Maurice's predicament, introduced him to Jeffrey Furst.

In July, 1988, Jeffrey went over to Maurice's house, saw the set up, the studio, the group, learned they were with CBS Records, met Dick Scott and Mary, and the New Kids performed for him. Maurice and everybody gave a good performance, while asking for a $100,000 loan from Jeffrey's Mortgage Company. Jeff, the businessman, wanted security, and Maurice, having paid cash for his house years before, had no liens and no mortgage on his house. Jeffrey said okay. After he had appraised the house, he would take the risk, lend Maurice the $100,000, take a mortgage on the building and a percentage on the group. But, Maurice said no to the last item. He would not, after he put all that work into building the New Kids on the Block, give a piece of them to a guy he had just met. (No way, Jose!) and he meant it! Maurice was prepared to sell his house if he had to, before he would give up a major percentage of his group to a stranger. Jeff persisted, but Maurice remained firm, in the end Jeff relented and gave Maurice the $100,000, thinking and hoping that if the New Kids were successful, he would be able to reap some of the benefits by association. By the next summer, Maurice would pay Jeffrey back personally…..with interest. Jeff would do a concert with the New Kids, and his press would always read "J.D. Furst, the man who first helped the New Kids on the Block out."

The New Kids at the Boston Music Awards

In Los Angeles, a top forty radio programmer was making a lot of noise about the New Kids. He loved the album and video, and was not adverse to calling up everybody, telling them the Gospel Truth that this group was made for top forty radio. Meanwhile Maurice had the $100,000 and gave the money to the right people. The money was spread around; and before you could say "one, two, three, four, five, ladies and gentlemen, boys and girls"; the New Kids on the Block were on top forty radio all over the country. "You Got The Right Stuff", "I'll Be Loving You (Forever)", "Cover Girl". Please, Don't Go Girl" .....those songs were on their way to becoming the most requested radio songs in the world. "Hanging Tough", the album and single would smash many, many Billboard and Cashbox chart records.

And, Maurice Starr's toes would twinkle when "Hanging Tough" would become the first top-five album by a teen group since the

Jackson 5 did it in 1970. The album and singles would go to number one many times. But, the beginning, boys and girls, was Tiffany. Tiffany, a very pretty teenage pop star was riding 4 million in album sales, beginning with an early Tommy James and the Shondells song. "I Think We're Alone Now". The ideal "mall girl", she was the idol of pre-teen and teen suburban mall girls. With the new thrust of the CBS pop marketing and promotion departments, people were beginning to listen to Maurice and Dick.

And a meeting was set up between Dick Scott and Tiffany's management. Things worked out between them, and this, boys and girls is what happened. "I was doing a concert, and my agent comes in" recalls Tiffany. "He said, 'There's this new group called the New Kids on the Block, and they're here tonight. They want to come in and perform for you in your dressing room!' I thought…..now? I'm eating! But then I remembered when I was twelve and I would audition for someone who was eating. And, they'd say 'That was really good.' Even though they weren't paying any attention. So, I just set my food aside and they came in…it was such a small room. And they had dance steps and everything—so they were hitting each other in the face! My girlfriend Sue was there, too. I met all of them and then Jerry, my agent, and George, my manager, said "Why don't we put them in the show tonight and just take a chance? They've got a tape. So why don't we just do it. 'They sing live to pre-recorded tapes. So they went into the show…It worked out because I have so many girls coming to my show. And now there were five incredibly cute guys up there! They were a lot of fun…even though they're guys!"

Well, in four months, Tiffany would open for the New Kids, in six months they would all go to Japan, tour across America, sell millions of albums, have millions upon millions of fans called "Block-heads!. Their concerts would sell-out in minutes, Dick Scott and Maurice Starr would buy out Mary Alford. But, with two albums, one on its way to selling 17 million copies, and the earlier one, now finally discovered by their legions of fans selling 4 million, and a Christmas album that sold 3 million copies, Mary Alford along with

A Step Closer

Dick Scott, Donnie Wahlberg, Jordan Knight, Jonathan Knight, Danny Wood, Joey McIntyre and their leader the General Maurice Starr would count their money, individually, in the millions and millions and millions and millions and millions of dollars.

Maurice Starr and Tony Rose laying down the tracks for NKOTB's album "Merry, Merry Christmas" at Hit City Recording Studio (Roxbury) – 1989

And the rest, Dear Boys and Girls is History:

You know the Story.

It begins:

Once upon a time....There were five boys: Donnie, Danny, Jordan, Jonathan, and Joey...and A guy named Maurice Starr....

The Rise of New Kids on the Block...

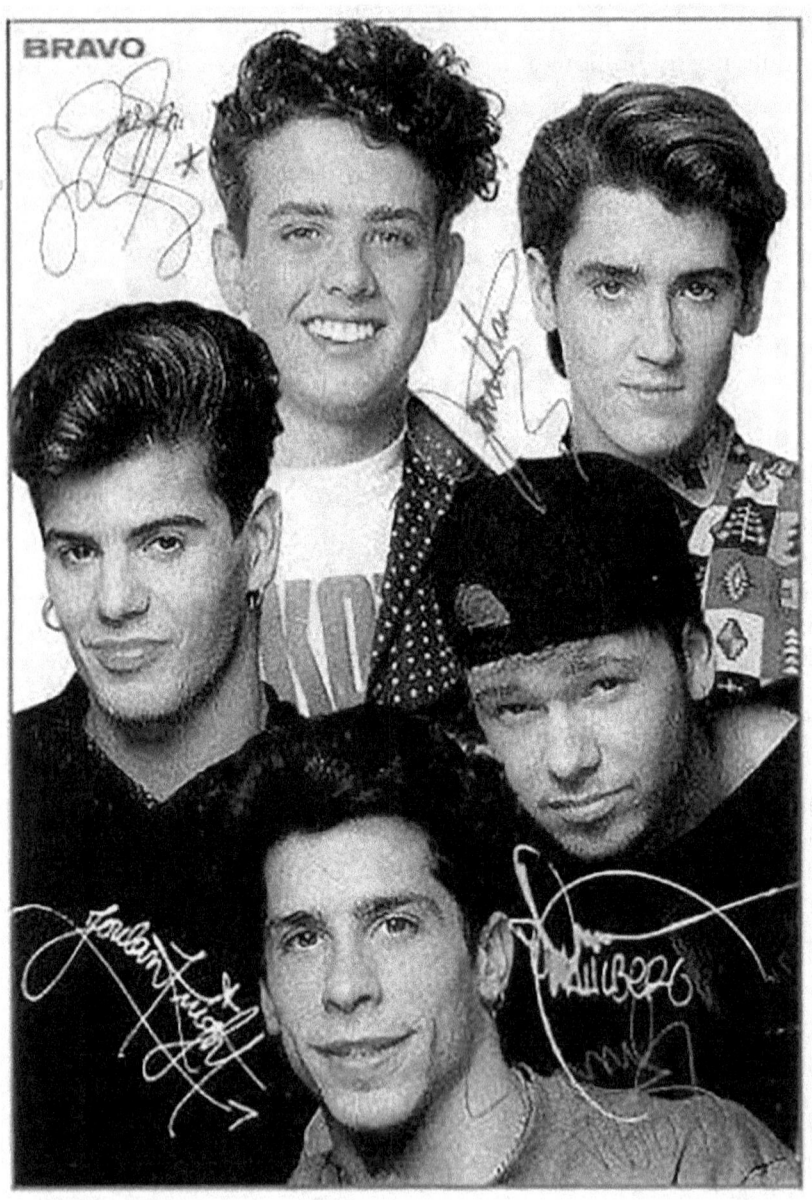

Conclusion

In 1994, The New Kids on the Block split up on amicable terms. Before breaking up, NKOTB was a worldwide phenomenon, selling more than 70 million albums and they topped *Forbes* magazine's list of highest paid American entertainers—above both Michael Jackson and Madonna. They also became the first American group to achieve 6 top 5 hits in a row in the UK.

Mark Wahlberg and Donnie Wahlberg perform as Marky Mark & the Funky Bunch

Donnie Wahlberg shared time on stage with his brother, Mark Wahlberg, formerly known as rapper "Marky Mark" of Marky Mark and the Funky Bunch. Mark is now an Academy-award nominated actor and television producer. Donnie Wahlberg went on to follow his brother Mark's career path and won several acting roles including the man who shot Bruce Willis at the start of "The Sixth Sense", and in the TV series "Boomtown". Joe McIntyre appeared on the BBC2 TV show "Never Mind The Buzzcocks". In 2002, he started acting in the drama series "Boston Public" playing a teacher. He continues to record, tour, and dance—in 2006 he was on ABC's "Dancing With the Stars". Jonathan Knight appeared on the Oprah Winfrey show in 2001 and now works in real estate as a developer in the Boston area; Jordan Knight still records and made a regrettable appearance on "The Surreal life". Danny Wood is a music producer.

The reunited New Kids on the Block officially released their new single "Summertime" on May 13, 2008. Sweet and bright, the song has a great '80s vibe that can be enjoyed by everyone, at every age. The New Kids On The Block have also penciled in a September 8, 2008 date for a new album, which will be released by Interscope.

Conclusion

Just when you thought the New Kids on the Block reunion couldn't get any sweeter, word comes that the guys are recording a song with another favorite boy band from Boston: New Edition. Days after New Edition took home the Golden Note Award, presented to them by the "General" Maurice Starr at the 21st annual ASCAP Rhythm & Soul awards in Beverly Hills, the group (minus Bobby Brown) went into an L.A. studio to record with the New Kids on the Block. The ensemble track, titled "Full Service," will appear on New Kids On The Block's not-yet-titled upcoming album.

Maurice Starr with New Edition at the 21st annual ASCAP Rhythm & Soul Awards (2008)

Legendary music mogul and mega-hit record producer, Maurice "The General" Starr is respected around the world for spearheading the contemporary boy band era. He has generated multi-platinum sales of more than 500 million units. In association with New Kids, Starr's name can be found in the Guinness Book of World Records for his sold-out concerts everywhere. He is mentioned on more than one million pages of the Internet, for discovering, producing, promoting and managing two of the biggest and most successful teen acts in the history of the entertainment business.

In 1993, Maurice Starr departed the field of pop music for gospel; and late in the year, he left New England for Atlanta. Starr formed General Entertainment Management, an all-purpose management and production company on which he managed and produced such acts as: Rick Wes, Perfect Gentlemen, and the Superiors and shortly thereafter, he relocated to his hometown of Deland, Florida. Since that time, Starr has formed Maurice Starr Productions, written back-to-back hit songs

The Rise of New Kids on the Block...

and worked for countless acts including: LL Cool J, Mariah Carey, P. Diddy, Mase, Kurt Franklin, Patti Labelle, Luther Vandross, Roberta Flack, Ricky Martin, Bow Wow and Lil Romeo, just to name a few.

Tony Rose, Publisher/CEO, Amber Communications Group, Inc., Former Record Producer, Record Company Executive, and Maurice Starr, Founder, Producer, New Edition, New Kids On The Block and The Heartbeat Boys, Celebrate together at Maurice Starr's 25th Year World Famous Hollywood Talent Night, November 11-12, 2005, Daytona Beach, FL

In 2005 a story in *The Orlando Sentinel* newspaper, announced that Maurice Starr was planning to form a new group in the style of his original super group, New Kids On The Block, soon to be named HeartBeat Boys. Starr assembled the best entertainment dream team money could buy, in order to develop the newly recruited members of the HeartBeat Boys into superstar artists and predicts that they will be the biggest teen act in the history of the entertainment business. The HeartBeat Boys' upcoming 2008 debut CD release is entitled, "From The Heart". (www.heartbeatboys.com)

In the spring of 2008 a collaboration of the Super Producer Maurice Starr (the General) and the Radio Broadcast Maverick Chris Hill (the Captain) is the first of many Internet Broadcast projects for STARR98.com, a station designed specifically to showcase all the music genres that Maurice Starr has produced and collaborated on from Gospel to Pop, from Hip Hop to R & B.

For further information, go to: www.mauricestarronline.com

New Kids On the Block Albums & Singles

Produced By Maurice Starr (1986 - 1991)

The Rise of New Kids on the Block...

New Kids on the Block is the self-titled debut album, released in the spring of 1986, but went commercially unnoticed. Three years later, as a result of the success of their second album (*Hangin' Tough*), Columbia Records released the *New Kids on the Block* track "Didn't I (Blow Your Mind)". Subsequently the albums sales spiked, and *New Kids on the Block* eventually went 3x platinum.

Track listing
1. "Stop It Girl"
2. "Didn't I (Blow Your Mind)"
3. "Popsicle"
4. "Angel"
5. "Be My Girl"
6. "New Kids on the Block"
7. "Are You Down?"
8. "I Wanna Be Loved by You"
9. "Don't Give Up On Me"
10. "Treat Me Right"

Singles
"Be My Girl," April 1986
"Stop It Girl," July 1986
" Didn't I (Blow Your Mind)," August 1989

Hangin' Tough is the second album from New Kids on the Block. By the end of 1989, *Hangin' Tough* had become the #1 album in America, spun off five top ten hits (two #1 singles), went 8x platinum in the US and ended up selling 16 million copies worldwide. In January 1990, the album won two American Music Awards for 'Favorite Pop/Rock Album' and 'Favorite Pop/Rock Band/Duo/Group.'

Track listing
1. "You Got It (The Right Stuff)"
2. "Please Don't Go Girl"
3. "I'll Be Loving You (Forever)"
4. "Cover Girl"
5. "I Need You"
6. "Hangin' Tough"
7. "I Remember When"
8. "What'cha Gonna Do (About It)"
9. "My Favorite Girl"
10. "Hold On"

Singles
"Please Don't Go Girl" - April 1988
"You Got It (The Right Stuff)" - November 1988
"I'll Be Loving You (Forever)" - April 1989
"Hangin' Tough" - July 1989
"Cover Girl" - September 1989
"My Favorite Girl" - January 1990

The Rise of New Kids on the Block...

Merry, Merry Christmas is the third album, released in the United States by Columbia Records on September 19, 1989. It went double platinum and spawned the top ten single, "This One's for the Children."

Track listing
1. "This One's for the Children"
2. "Last Night I Saw Santa Claus"
3. "I'll Be Missin You Come Christmas (A Letter to Santa)"
4. "I Still Believe In Santa Claus"
5. "Merry, Merry Christmas"
6. "The Christmas Song"
7. "Funky, Funky Xmas"
8. "White Christmas"
9. "The Little Drummer Boy"
10. "This One's for the Children (Reprise)"

Singles
This One's For The Children October 1989
Funky, Funky Xmas December 1989

Step by Step is the fourth album, released in June 1990 and debuting at #1 on the Billboard Pop Albums chart and at #1 on the UK Albums Chart, with the leadoff title track single topping the charts simultaneously and selling nearly three million copies, making it their highest selling single. Another top ten single, "Tonight", followed with just over a million copies sold.

Track listing
1. "Step by Step"
2. "Tonight"
3. "Baby, I Believe In You"
4. "Call It What You Want"
5. "Let's Try It Again"
6. "Happy Birthday"
7. "Games"
8. "Time Is On Our Side"
9. "Where Do I Go from Here?"
10. "Stay With Me Baby"
11. "Funny Feeling"
12. "Never Gonna Fall In Love Again"

Singles
"Step By Step" - released May 1990
"Tonight" - released June 1990
"Let's Try It Again"
"Valentine Girl"

The Rise of New Kids on the Block...

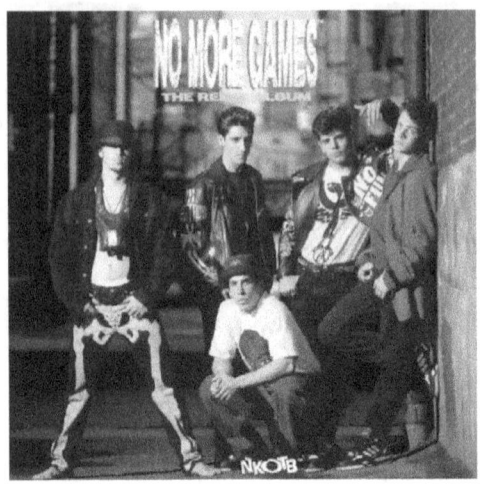

No More Games/The Remix Album, released in 1991is the fifth album from pop group New Kids on the Block, and their first 'hits' compilation. It was certified Gold in the U.S.

Track listing
1. "Games [The Kids Get Hard Mix]"
2. "Call It What You Want [The C&C Pump-It Mix]"
3. "Please Don't Go Girl"
4. "Cover Girl"
5. "Baby, I Believe In You [The Love Mix]"
6. "Hangin' Tough [In a Funky Way]"
7. "Step by Step [The C&C Vocal Club Mix]"
8. "My Favorite Girl"
9. "Valentine Girl [The C&C Quiet Storm Mix]"
10. "The Right Stuff [The New Kids in the House Mix]"
11. "Whatcha Gonna Do (About It)"
12. "Never Gonna Fall In Love Again [The C&C Music Factory Mix]"

Singles
Games
Call It What You Want

Let The Touring Begin:

Sep 18, 08 / Toronto, ON / AIR CANADA CENTER
Sep 19, 08 / Toronto, ON / AIR CANADA CENTER
Sep 20, 08 / Montreal, QB / BELL CENTRE
Sep 21, 08 / Toronto, ON / AIR CANADA CENTER
Sep 23, 08 / East Rutherford, NJ / IZOD CENTER
Sep 24, 08 / Uniondale, NY / NASSAU VETERANS MEMORIAL COLISEUM
Sep 26, 08 / Boston, MA / TD BANKNORTH GARDEN
Sep 27, 08 / Atlantic City, NJ / BORGATA HOTEL/CASINO EVENT CENTER
Sep 28, 08 / Boston, MA / TD BANKNORTH GARDEN
Sep 30, 08 / Uncasville, CT / MOHEGAN SUN ARENA
Oct 02, 08 / Washington, DC / VERIZON CENTER
Oct 03, 08 / Cleveland, OH / QUICKEN ARENA
Oct 04, 08 / Chicago, IL / ALLSTATE ARENA
Oct 08, 08 / Los Angeles, CA / STAPLES CENTER
Oct 10, 08 / San Jose, CA / HP PAVILION
Oct 11, 08 / Las Vegas, NV / MANDALAY BAY

The Rise of New Kids on the Block...

Oct 13, 08 / Glendale, AZ / JOBING.COM ARENA
Oct 16, 08 / Houston, TX / TOYOTA CENTER
Oct 17, 08 / San Antonio, TX / ATT CENTER
Oct 18, 08 / New Orleans, LA / NEW ORLEANS ARENA
Oct 19, 08 / Dallas, TX / AMERICAN AIRLINES CENTER
Oct 21, 08 / Minneapolis, MN / XCEL ENERGY CENTER
Oct 22, 08 / Milwaukee, WI / BRADLEY CENTER
Oct 24, 08 / Chicago, IL / ALLSTATE ARENA
Oct 25, 08 / Detroit, MI / PALACE OF AUBURN HILLS
Oct 27, 08 / New York, NY / MADISON SQUARE GARDEN
Oct 29, 08 / Atlanta, GA / GWINNETT CENTER
Nov 01, 08 / Ft. Lauderdale, FL / BANKATLANTIC CENTER
Nov 02, 08 / Tampa, FL / ST. PETE TIMES FORUM
Nov 05, 08 / Philadelphia, PA / WACHOVIA CENTER
Nov 06, 08 / Providence, RI / DUNKIN' DONUTS CENTER
Nov 10, 08 / St. Louis, MO / SCOTTRADE CENTER
Nov 11, 08 / Kansas City, MO / SPRINT CENTER
Nov 12, 08 / Omaha, NE / QUEST CENTER
Nov 14, 08 / Denver, CO / BROOMFIELD EVENT CENTER
Nov 15, 08 / Salt Lake City, UT / E CENTER/UNITED
Nov 18, 08 / Edmonton, AB / REXALL PLACE
Nov 19, 08 / Calgary, AB / SADDLEDOME
Nov 21, 08 / Vancouver, BC / GENERAL MOTORS PLACE
Nov 22, 08 / Seattle, WA / KEY ARENA/TACOMA DOME
Nov 23, 08 / Portland, OR / ROSE GARDEN ARENA
Nov 25, 08 / San Diego, CA / COX ARENA
Nov 26, 08 / Los Angeles, CA / STAPLES CENTER

Index

The index has been organized by first name for ease of finding references

20 Linwood Square 65, 72, 76, 80, 82-83, 103-104, 106, 108
233 East Howry Avenue 65
27 Dudley Street 33, 109

A
A & M Records 123
Aerosmith 65, 73
Africa Bambatta 91, 93
Ahmad Jamal 38
Ahmet Ertegun 51
Allen Freed 70
All-Platinum Records 80
Ambitions 73
American Bandstand 45
American Legion Highway 103
"American Hot Wax" 70
Apollo Theater, The 53, 66, 114, 116, 129-131
Aretha Franklin 49, 51
Art Blakeley 38
Art Tatum 38
Arthur Baker 79, 85, 90-93, 95
Arthur Conway 51
Arthur Rayford 59, 64-65
Ashmont Station 20
Ashmont Street 21
Atlantic Records 51, 134

B
B.B King 38
"Baby Come On" 72, 74, 76
Baltimore 76
Barry Rosenthal 109
Basin Street 64
Bay State Banner xii
Beach Boys 51
Beatles, The 1, 49, 51-52
"Beat the Bush" 88
Belmont High 15
Ben's Lounge 101
Bernard Edwards 81
Berry Gordy 51-52, 69
Bessie Smith 38-39
BET 124, 127-128
Bethune-Cookman College 50
Big Step Management 119
Big Step Productions 118
Billie Eckstine 38
Billie Holiday 38
Bind Lemon Jefferson 38
Birdland 39
Black Rock 121
Blaze 90
Blue Hill Avenue 80
Bo Diddley 45, 47, 57
Bobby Brown 46, 87, 92, 98
Boston City Hospital 63
Boston International Recording Studio 82, 86
Boston International Records 70, 83-84, 86, 89, 92, 106
Boston Music Awards 98, 135
Boston Music Scene 61
Boston Public Schools 13
Boston Red Sox 2
"'Bout Time I Funk You" 71, 72, 74, 76
Boylston Street 64, 103
Brian Jones 51

The Rise of New Kids on the Block...

Bromley Heath Housing Project, The 96
Brook Payne 88
Brunswick Records 77
Buffalo 74, 76
Buffalo Civic Center 74

C

Cab Calloway 38
Calvin Johnson 37, 43, 47, 50, 57, 67, 69, 72, 74, 76, 109, 125
Cambridge 80
"Candy Girl" 89, 92,-93, 97
Carla Thomas 49
CBS Records 88, 114-115, 117, 119-120, 125, 134
Cecil Holmes 114, 120, 125
"Celebrity Award Shows" 85Capital Records 125
Charles Alexander xii, 74, 93
Charles Mingus 38
Charles Street Jail 21
Charlestown 14-15
Charlestown High 14-15
Charlie "Bird" Parker 38-39
Charlie Christian 38
Cheryl Sutton 114
Chess Brothers 85
Chess Records 39
Chicago. 39, 93
Chuck Berry 45, 57
City Hall 63
Clarence Paul 52
Cleveland 76
Club 51 xii, 79-80
Coasters 44
Codman Square 21
Columbia Records 39, 142, 144
Columbia Road 21
Concord-Carlisle High 15
Confunction 97
Copacabana Night Club 96
Coral Records 39
Corteez Lounge 80, 113
Count Basie 38-40

Count Basie Band 39-40
Curtis Blow 81
Cynthia Horner 96

D

"Dance Music Report" 90
Danny William Wood xi, xvii, xix, 1-2, 6-7, 9-10, 15-16, 21-26, 33, 47, 64, 89, 109-110, 112, 115-116, 121, 123-124, 127-130, 137, 140
Daytona Beach 40, 50
Daytona Beach Community College 50
Deland, Florida xi, 40, 50, 58, 65, 74, 85
Detroit 51-52, 69, 130
Dial Records 39
Diana Ross 51, 69
Dick Scott 52, 69, 113, 119, 121, 124, 134, 136-137
Dinah Washington 38
Disney 40-41
Dizzie Gillespie 38
Doc's xii, 64, 78, 98
Donna Summer 65
Donnie Johnson 70, 109
Donnie Wahlberg xi, xvii, xix, 1-2, 5-10, 15-17, 21-22, 24-26, 28, 33, 38, 43, 47, 63, 67, 69, 74, 76, 89, 108-110, 112-113, 115-116, 118-119, 121, 123-124, 127-130, 137, 139-140
Donovan 51
Doo Drop Inn Lounge 56
Doors 1, 39, 51
Dorchester xi, xvii, xix, 1-2, 5-7, 9, 12-16, 20-23, 25-26, 63, 65, 79, 86, 96, 103, 106, 108, 112, 124, 130
Dorchester Avenue 21-22
Dorchester Court House 21-22
Dorchester High 1, 13
Dr. Funkenchain 79
Duke Ellington 38
Duke Jordan 39

E

Earl "Fatha" Hines 38
Electric Power Band 78, 80
Ella Fitzgerald 38
Ellen Jackson 15
Elroy R.C. Smith 119, 125
Elvin Rayford 37-38, 43, 45, 47, 53, 57-58, 67, 72, 76, 82, 84, 109, 125
Elvis Presley 8, 45
Energetics 73
Englewood 81
Entrigue 9, 79-80, 101-102
Eric Nuri 79, 114
Estelle's 64

F

Fats Domino 45
"Fever In The Funkhouse" 76
Filmore East 51
Filmore West 51
"Flaming Starr" 76
Footlight Club 29-32
Four Tops 51, 116
Frankie Crocker 129
Franklin Park 115
Funky Bunch 139-140
"Funky Worm" 84
Furious Five 81

G

"Gang War" 88
Gary, Indiana 52
Gheryl Busby 96-97
Giants Stadium xix
Gladys Knight and The Pips 52
"Good Golly Miss Molly" 70
Gordon Worthy 67, 73, 91, 118, 134
Grandmaster Flash 81
Grateful Dead, The 51
Growler-Deland High School 44

H

Hal Jackson 129-130, 133
"Hangin Tough" 98, 130
Harold Melvin and the Bluenotes 58
Harvey Fuqua 52
Holland/ Dozier and Holland 52
Hollywood Talent Night 85-86, 113
Hollywood Talent Show 9
Huddie Ledbetter ("Leadbelly") 38
Hyde Park 14-15
Hyde Park High 14-15
Hypnotics, The 79

I

Ink Spots 38
Inner City Broadcasting 114, 129
Intergalactic Recording Studios 90
Intermediate Recording Studio 67, 75
"In the Streets" 12, 74
Isaac Hayes 49
Isley Brothers 52

J

J. Geils Band 65, 73
J. J. Johnson 52
J. Jizzon 22
Jackie McLean 38
Jackson Five 5, 53, 55, 88-89, 104, 125, 136
James Brown 49, 51, 57-58, 67, 117
Jamie Kelly 109
Janis Joplin 51
Jazz Workshop 64
Jazzy J 90
Jefferson Airplane 51
Jeffrey Furst 133-134
Jeremiah Burke 1, 13
Jim Morrison 51-52
Jimi Hendrix 1, 49, 51-52
Jimmy Page 50
Joe McIntyre xix, 110, 140
Joe Tex 49, 78
Joey McIntyre 34, 89, 137
John Coltrane 38
John Luongo 88
Johnson Brothers 43, 48, 52, 55-59, 65-67, 69-70, 72-74, 78, 80, 82-83, 87, 89, 103-104, 108, 117, 126
Johnson Family 37, 39, 41, 43

151

Jonathan Rashleigh Knight xi, xvii, xix, 1-2, 6-7, 10-12, 15-16, 19-22, 25-26, 28, 33, 47, 64, 89, 109-110, 112, 116, 121, 124, 127-130, 137, 140

Jonzun Crew 92-93, 103

Jordan Nathaniel Marcel Knight xi, xix, 1-2, 6-7, 10-13, 15-17, 19-22, 25-26, 28, 33, 39, 47, 64, 89, 109-110, 112, 116, 121, 123-124, 127-130, 137-140

Joseph Mulrey McIntyre 27-28

Judge Garrity 13-14

Junior Walker and the All Stars 52

K

Kansas City 39

Kathy Jacobson 92

Keith Jackson 74

Kraftwork 91

L

Lakeside 74

Larkin Arnold 114-115, 118-119

Larry "Woo" Wedgeworth 73, 79

Lawrence "Larry" Johnson xi, xviii, 5, 9-10, 34, 37-38, 40, 42-47, 49-50, 52-53, 55, 57-58, 64-67, 69-84, 87, 89, 91-93, 98, 103, 106-109, 118, 123, 125, 134

Led Zeppelin 50

Leslie Jones 101-102

Lester Young 38

Lewis West 78

Lexington High 15

Lionel Hampton 38-40, 43-44, 46

Lionel Hampton Orchestra 39-40

Lisa Lisa and the Cult Jam 116

Little Richard 45, 69-70, 87

Livingston Taylor 65-66

London xii, 52, 77

Los Angeles 52, 97, 102-103, 114, 135

"Lost in Space" 93, 103

Louie's Lounge 64

Louis Armstrong 38

Luther Ingram 78

M

M.E.T.C.O. 15

Ma Rainey 38

Madison Park High 13

Madison Square Garden 77

Madonna 139

Mamas and Papas 51

Margo Thunder 9, 79-80, 101-102, 127-128

Mark Wahlberg 109, 139-140

Mark Weiner 106, 109

Marlene and Allen Knight 15, 19

Martha and The Vandellas 52

Marvelettes 51

Marvin Gaye 51, 58, 64

Mary Alford 9, 25, 33, 79, 101-102, 106-107, 118-119, 124, 136

Mary Wells 51

Massachusetts Avenue 80

Massachusetts State Lottery 69

Mattapan 1, 13, 65

Maurice Starr xi-xii, xvii-xix, 6, 9-10, 17, 22, 25, 28, 33-35, 37, 41, 53, 58, 64, 67, 69-73, 75-78, 80, 84-87, 89-90, 92-93, 95-98, 101, 103-130, 133-137, 141

Maurice Starr Productions 118

Max Roach 38-39

Mayor Kevin White 1, 14, 63

MCA Records 96-97

Melbourne Street 22

Menudo xiii, xvii

Mercury Records 39

Metro Records 39

Michael Bivens 87, 93

Michael Jackson xviii, 9-10, 34, 108, 139

Mick Jagger 51

Mickey and Silvia 80

Midnight Star 74

Miles Davis 38-39

Mills Brothers 38

Miracles 51

Mission Control 103, 118, 123
Moments. 81
"More Bounce To The Ounce" 84
Morris Levy 85
Motown 52, 69, 88, 114
MTV 124, 127
Muddy Waters 38
Muhammed Ali 72

N

Nat King Cole 38, 110
Neighborhood Children's Theater 30
New Edition xii, 9, 17, 33, 46, 53, 87-91, 93, 95-97, 103-104, 106-108, 115, 121
New Kids on the Block xi-xii, xiv, xviii, xx, 2, 4, 6, 8, 10, 12, 14, 16, 18, 20, 22, 24, 26, 28, 30, 32, 34, 36, 38, 40-42, 44, 46, 48, 50, 52, 54, 56, 58, 60, 62, 64, 66, 68, 70, 72, 74, 76, 78, 79, 80, 82, 84, 86, 88, 90, 92, 94, 96, 98, 100-102, 104, 106-108, 110, 112, 114, 116-120, 122-124, 126-128, 130-132, 134-136, 137, 138-140, 142-144, 146, 148
New Orleans 39
Newton-Wellesley High 15
Nile Rodgers 81
Norman Whitfield 52
North Dorchester xi, xix, 1-2, 6-7, 9, 12-13, 15, 20-21, 23, 26, 79, 103, 106, 108, 124, 130
Northampton Street 64
Northeastern University 96
Nynuk 111, 113, 115-116

O

Lane's 101
Ohio Players 84
Orchard Park Community Center 96
Orchard Park Projects 85-87
Orlando 40-41
Osmonds 104
Otis Redding 49, 51, 78

P

"Pac Jam" 92
Parker Street Lounge 69
Parliament Funkadelics 71
Paul McCraven 92
Paul's Mall 64
Percy Sutton 114
Phaedra Butler 125, 127
Picture Perfect 134
"Planet Rock" 91, 92, 93
Platters 44
Posse-Spring Records 90
Prince Charles and the City Beat Band xii, 74, 77, 79-80, 88, 93, 102
Providence 71-72
Puff McCloud 22

R

Ralph Tresvant 87, 93, 95
Ray Charles 38
Ray Harris 74-75
Ray Johnson, Jr. 43, 58
Ray Johnson, Sr. 74
Rayford 43, 50-51, 56, 59, 64-65, 78, 82, 85, 90-93, 95-96
RCA 72-76, 101-102
Richard "Dimples" Fields 101
Ricky Bell 93
"Right On!" Magazine 96
Rise Club 80
Robert Plant 50
Rock and Roll 45, 58
"Rockers Revenge" 92
Roger Trotman 84
Rolling Stones 49, 51
Ronald Devoe 90
Roscoe Gorham 64, 73, 75, 84-85, 91-92, 127
Roscoe's 64, 79-80, 85-87, 92, 101, 108
Roulette Records 85
Roxbury Music Scene xi
Royal School 16
Rufus Thomas 49
Run DMC 8
Ruth Brown 44

153

S

Sam and Dave 49, 51
San Francisco 51
Sarah Vaughan 38
Sargent Funk 79
Savoy Records 39
Savoy, The 39
Screamin' Jay Hawkins 45
Seminole County Public Schools 50
Shalamar 74
Shanty's 64
"She's Got Papers On Me" 101
Simon and Garfunkel 51
"Slippin and Slidin" 70
Sly 47, 49, 51, 57, 88, 93
Sly and the Family Stone 47, 51
Slyck 88, 93
Smokey Robinson 51-52
Solid Platinum Records 74, 88
Soul-Sonic Force 91
South Boston 1-2, 6, 14-15, 33, 109
South Boston High 14-15
South End Boy's Club 96
Spinners 52
Spotlight Records 39
St. Elizabeth's Parish 15
Stax 51
Steve Crumbley 71, 119
Steven Machat 88, 97
Stevie Wonder 52
Strand Theater 86, 113
Streetwise Records 92, 95-96, 106
Stylistics 97
Sugar Hill Gang 81-82
"Sugar Hill Rap" 81
Sugar Hill Records 81
Sugar Shack 64
Supremes 51
Sweet Mountain Studios 81
Sylvia Robinson 80, 82

T

Talbot Avenue 21
Tammy Terrell 52
Technical High School 13
Temptations 51
"The Scoop" 12
Thomas and Kay McIntyre 27, 32
Tiffany 136
Tom Silverman 85, 90-93, 103
Tommy Boy Records 85, 90-92, 103, 123
Tommy Porter 39
Tone Loc 81
Tony Rose xi-xiii, xix, 86, 93, 98, 137
"Trans Europe Express" 91
Travis Gorham 88
Tremont Street 64
"Tutti Fruitti" 70
Tyrone Davis 52, 78
Tyrone Procter 112

U

United Cerebral Palsy 113, 116

V

Virgin Records 102

W

W.I.L.D. 71, 119
Wanda Perry 79, 101-102
Warren Street 13, 80, 85
Washington Street 21-22, 80
"We Come To Jam" 90
Wembley Stadium 77
WERS 72
Wes 51, 67, 78, 103
WILD 72, 87, 92, 125
"Wild Thing" 81
William Trotter Middle Schools 13
Willie Mae Johnson 37, 118, 127
Woo/Worthy Productions 73
WRBB 72
WTBS 72
WUNR 72

Y

Yvonne Rose xiii, 80, 129
Yvonne Willis 80

Z

Zapp 84

ORDER FORM

WWW.NEWKIDSBOOK.COM

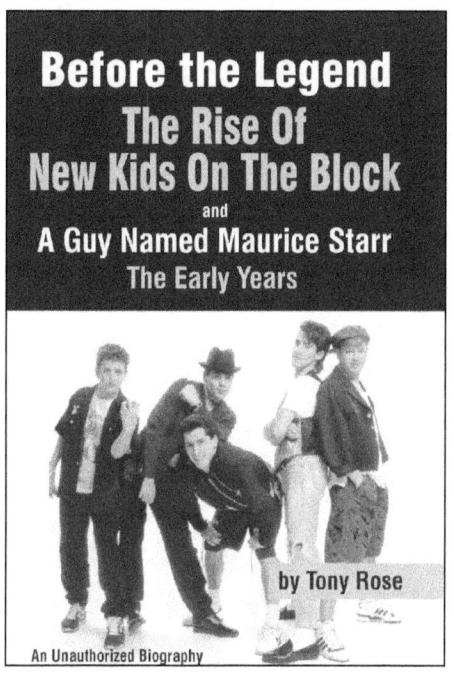

Online Orders:
WWW.NEWKIDSBOOK.COM

Postal Orders
Please Make Checks or Money Orders
Payable to "Amber Books"

Mail to
Colossus Books
1334 E. Chandler Blvd.
Suite 5-D67
Phoenix, AZ 85048

ORDER NOW—$15.00

Name:_____
Company Name:_____
Address:_____
City:_____ State:_____ Zip:_____
Telephone: (___) _____ E-mail:_____

New Kids on the Block	$15.00	
Black Eyed Peas	$16.95	
Red Hot Chili Peppers	$16.95	
Dr. Dre In the Studio	$16.95	
Kanye West	$16.95	
Tupac Shakur	$16.95	
Jay-Z…	$16.95	
Your Body's Calling Me:	$16.95	
Ready to Die: Notorious B.I.G.	$16.95	
Suge Knight:	$21.95	
50 Cent: No Holds Barred,	$16.95	
Aaliyah—An R&B Princess	$10.95	
Dr. Dre & Eminem	$10.95	
Divas of the New Millenium,	$16.95	
Michael Jackson: The King of Pop	$29.95	
The House that Jack Built	$16.95	

❏ Check ❏ Money Order ❏ Cashiers Check
❏ Credit Card: ❏ MC ❏ Visa ❏ Amex ❏ Discover

CC#_____
Expiration Date:_____
Payable to:
   Amber Books
   1334 E. Chandler Blvd., Suite 5-D67
   Phoenix, AZ 85048

Shipping: $5.00 per book. Allow 7 days for delivery.
Sales Tax: Add 7.05% to books shipped to Arizona addresses.

Total enclosed: $_____

WWW.AMBERBOOKS.COM

The Rise of New Kids on the Block...

Tony Rose, President of Solid Platinum Records & Productions and Maurice Starr, President of Boston International Records – 1989

The Rise of New Kids on the Block...

Tony Rose is the 2013 NAACP Image Award Winner for Outstanding Literature

About the Author

Tony Rose, Circa 1989

Tony Rose is the Publisher and CEO of Phoenix, AZ based, Amber Communications Group, Inc., the nation's largest African-American Publisher of Self-Help Books and Music Biographies. He is the 2013 44th Annual *NAACP Image Award Winner for Outstanding Literature and* The Harlem Book Fair / Phillis Wheatley Book Awards *"2013 African American Book Publisher of the Year"*.

ACGI's imprints include: The NAACP Image Awards winning, Amber Books Publishing; Amber Classics Books—Self-Help Reference Books; Colossus Books—Music Biographies; Amber/Wiley Books—Self Help and Financial Books Co-Published with John Wiley & Sons Inc.; Joyner/Amber Books—Co-Publishing with the Tom Joyner Foundation and Desmoon Books—Fiction.

Tony Rose was born in Roxbury (Boston) Massachusetts, raised in the Whittier Street Housing Projects, was honorably discharged from the U.S. Air Force after serving in the Vietnam War, and attended the University of Massachusetts and the University of California in Los Angeles. He was employed as a production assistant at the Burbank Studios (Warner Brothers and Columbia Pictures), in the accounting and sales division at Warner/Electra/Atlantic

Records (WEA), an accounts representative at Warren Lanier Public Relations and as an A & R representative at RCA Records, Los Angeles, California.

Rose returned to Boston and along with record producer Maurice Starr became the primary architect of that, which in the late 70's and 80's would be called "The Boston Black Music Scene" a movement that ultimately led to the discovery of the international blockbusters Prince Charles and the City Beat Band, The Jonzun Crew, New Edition, and New Kids on the Block. In 1979 he formed Solid Platinum Records and Productions and in 1982 he was named one of the "Top Ten Record Producers in the World". Rose in the 80's held recording / production deals with Virgin Records, Atlantic Records and Pavilion / CBS/Sony Records.

Rose was a successful Record Producer, Record Company Owner, Personal Manager, Music Publisher, Recording Studio Owner, Recording Engineer, Song Writer and Composer for more than fifteen years. His Solid Platinum Records and Productions was the first African American production company to have a production deal with Virgin Records. In 1983, albums produced by Rose *"Gang War"* and *"Stone Killers"* by Prince Charles and the City Beat Band reached Gold Album status and shared the charts with Michael Jackson's Thriller for six consecutive months in the number one, two and three positions throughout the world and his legendary "Prince Charles and the City Beat Band" albums *"Gang War"*, *"Stone Killers"*, *"Combat Zone"* and singles, have accounted for more than Four Million sold worldwide. Rose's many music awards include "Gold" and "Platinum" Albums and "Ampex Golden Reel" Awards for recording and engineering New Kids on the Block. Rose, has also penned *Before the Legend—The Rise of New Kids on the Block* and *...A Guy Named Maurice Starr—The Early Years*.

Tony Rose is the editor of numerous books and the co-writer of the national best-seller, *Is Modeling For You: The Handbook and Guide For The Young Aspiring Black Model,* written with Yvonne Rose; has penned the critically acclaimed, best-seller, *Before the Legend: The Rise of New Kids On The Block and A Guy Named Maurice Starr, The Early Years;* and has recently compiled, edited and published the award winning, *African American History In The United States of America—An Anthology—From Africa To President Barack Obama, Volume One*, a Top Ten Best African American Book.

Tony Rose Being Interviewed About Maurice Starr on YouTube
(scan the disc with your camera)

Forty years later, Award-Winning Record Producer and Book Publisher, Tony Rose, reflects on the Boston Music Scene

www.ingramcontent.com/pod-product-compliance
Lightning Source LLC
LaVergne TN
LVHW012019060526
838201LV00061B/4368